CW00486778

Adventures in Sober Land

...and how to live in Alcohol World

By

Simon Eastwood

Copyright © 2020 Simon Eastwood All rights reserved

No part of this book may be reproduced, or stored in a retrieval system, or transmitted in any form or by any means, electronic, mechanical, photocopying, recording, or otherwise, without express written permission of the publisher.

ISBN 9798616815521

Dedication

To my children

Contents

Introduction

I think it's important to say upfront that Sober Land is not actually a place. I sincerely apologise to those of you who thought I had discovered a Harry Potter-like world which could only be accessed by running into a wall on a station platform—something I did several times when I was drunk—and that this was all about my adventures fending off mythical creatures. The only creatures I have had to repel since arriving here are usually close family members or those within myself. No, Sober Land is more a virtual world or parallel existence that evolves in the mind and spreads outwards from there, superimposing itself onto the physical world.

It's rather trippy at first, which is quite ironic when you think about it. It's as if you've taken a sober pill of some sort, that first day you decide not to drink forever, and then suddenly find yourself transported into this HD-sharp world of rampaging feelings and giddy reality. And never far away, lurking in the undergrowth, those silent foes anxiety, depression and low self-esteem still watch on. They are of course why I emigrated to Alcohol World in the first place all those years ago, and they continue to make their presence felt. But living here in Sober Land allows me to spot them early, to head them off before they leap out from their hiding places and try to take me prisoner once again.

I think I now have a handle on living life here, nearly a year after stopping drinking, but even now, as I begin to write about my adventures, it continues to throw up some extraordinary experiences. So, I would love to share these experiences with you, these adventures. My intention is not to be indulgent but rather to tell you about the hilarious, challenging and exhilarating experiences of my journey from Alcohol World to Sober Land. Of living life both with and without using a mind-altering, mood-enhancing drug. To give you a sense of how much smaller and more fragile Sober Land is in comparison to Alcohol World, and how it often finds itself being attacked on all sides, largely by temptation but also by social expectation. As a collective, those in Sober Land have had to learn some pretty neat tricks in self-preservation: ducking and diving and holding on with resolute belief to Sober Land's systems and culture. But for all its fragility, it is a hugely powerful and immeasurably more profound place to live. I think, deep down, Alcohol World knows this, and that can be threatening. Particularly to those who own and promote Alcohol World as well as those who can't imagine life without it.

2

There is no magic formula to giving up alcohol, of course—
nor any drug you have become dependent on, for that
matter. However, reading books written by others who'd
already managed to cross that bridge before me helped to
build the crucial layers of conviction and courage to finally
do so myself. Watching countless Ted Talks and Vlogs,
YouTube videos and films all inspired me to engage with a
singularity of mind that was essential to my recovery. Being
part of a private online community of like-minded people,
which I discuss later in the book, was the cement that held
me together during tough times, and still does. At its core,
the key to my success in staying sober this time (where so
often I had failed) was to want to be free more than I
wanted anything else.

In that regard, I hope my experiences in some way help to
nudge you along a little further towards the bridge which I
have now crossed, if this is what you wish, while also
offering some amusement as you make your way. I mean,
we have to be able to laugh, don't we? Particularly at
ourselves and the sheer nonsense that emanates from
what we say and do sometimes. Life is incredibly funny if
you look at it from the right angle.

However, above all else, my primary reason for stopping drinking was my children. They were what finally enabled me to climb out from the cold, cold clutches of dependency, when I thought it wasn't possible. I just could not face the possible consequences anymore of continuing along the path I'd trodden for so long. They are still my motivation and I don't think I need to say why. After all, I would only embarrass them if I used a certain word beginning with the letter L. WOULDN'T I, CHILDREN? Sorry, that's a severe example of 'embarrassing dad', but I couldn't resist.

Finally, I want to say something about my wife. I realise, as I look back on what I have written, that my references to her might appear quite stark. They may give the impression that I lack any feelings of warmth towards her, but that is not true. We have been through a huge amount together and alcohol has not been our friend, though we thought it was for many years. We are now in the process of separating, kindly and considerately, and I continue to be very fond of her and to be her friend. So, when I describe moments where she appears in these adventures, my purpose has been to add context rather than to go into the details of my relationship with her. It all feels too raw and pertinent to do it any other way, but my intention is never to be cold or critical. We both love our children beyond measure and all we want is the very best for them.

4

Anyway, just before we move to Chapter 1, I wanted to show you something I wrote in the early stages of sobriety about the different phases I found myself having moved through. It's a pretty quick read but now, all this time later, I realise it was the catalyst for writing this book.

Finally accepting those uncomfortable feelings.

At the time of writing this I am almost six months free of alcohol, so relatively speaking I have only just arrived here in Sober Land. It's really rather lovely but daunting still as I try to acclimatise to what are very different weather conditions (temperate), customs (based on compassion) and ways of living (courageous).

I feel that by disclosing the following thoughts I am being somewhat presumptuous, considering my short time here, and I do have this superstitious feeling that by declaring them, this new home will suddenly disappear like a mirage and I will find myself once again back in that dark, cold and desperately claustrophobic place I tried to escape from for years.

But I am going to give this a go anyway as I really do wish this to be of help and for it to give hope to other people who have just landed in Sober Land, or who indeed might have been here for some time but are still grappling with a few things. Perhaps most of all though, this is for the people who are seriously considering making the journey here for the first time.

For me, there have been three key phases, two of which I've moved through and one I've recently entered, each to do with dealing with uncomfortable feelings. Please note that uncomfortable feelings are spread over a very wide spectrum of emotion from boredom to somewhat stressed, onto varying levels of anxiety and depression, then further along to deep hurt, anger and finally despair. Interestingly, the relatively mild feelings of boredom, and what I can only describe as a sense of emptiness, are a bit of a killer when it comes to wanting to reach for the bottle because they're everyday triggers. I do not underestimate them.

PHASE 1: AVOIDANCE

This went on for about thirty years, give or take. For the first twenty, I had no idea I was dealing with my feelings by using alcohol to self-medicate. I'd heard the phrase 'self-medication' being bandied around, but I really only understood it at a theoretical level: that people used alcohol to deal with their feelings.

I just didn't realise I was one of them. I mean, I sort of did, but not really. Not truly.

I knew I enjoyed the feelings alcohol brought because after a pint of lager or a glass of wine, that warm and fuzzy feeling replaced all other feelings. However, I didn't realise that I was actually trying to escape something, even if it was only boredom sometimes.

For the last ten years, I really knew something was up. The problem was that when those uncomfortable feelings came, it was just too easy not to face up to them. The abundant and socially acceptable alternative to sitting with my feelings was just so overwhelmingly tempting. The anaesthesia of alcohol had such an addictive pull and everywhere I turned it was, in fact, encouraged. What's more, nearly all my friends and colleagues appeared to be doing the same thing. Difficult to say no, really.

So, this phase 1 was a very long, drawn-out one which became more and more painful the more I practiced the art of avoidance. A terrible vicious circle, where the drug I used to deal with my feelings was either exacerbating those feelings or creating them in the first place. That's the problem with alcohol: like any powerful drug you're coming down from, it seriously depletes your mind, body, and spirit, creating its very own particular brand of anxiety and depression. It also wreaks havoc on any naturally driven uncomfortable feelings you already have. So, come early evening, you reach for the instant fix in a bottle and click repeat.

PHASE 2: DISTRACTION

This phase started the moment I stopped drinking and kicked in on that first evening. So, now we have the uncomfortable feelings coupled with the choice not to drink those feelings away. Help, what do I do? Well, like many others do, I ran full-on into a massive, messy pool of distractions in an agitated frenzy. Anything to take me away from obsessing about having a drink. Here are a few of the distractions. Putting my pyjamas on very early in the evening (I didn't do this in a frenzy) because, for me, pyjamas had this magical ability to trick my mind that I now wanted a cup of tea rather than a glass of wine. Thank you, pyjamas. I ate early instead of building up to my evening meal by consuming three large glasses of red wine as if I was in training for something. I unashamedly turned to alcohol-free lager, which I still love drinking. I read books on giving up alcohol, watched Ted Talks and YouTube videos on giving up alcohol, devoured blogs and articles about it, watched films where the central theme was about alcohol addiction and most importantly joined Club Soda, the Mindful Drinking Movement™.

A word about Club Soda. There, I can read and share posts in a secure and private online group with people who feel the same way as I do. I can attend events, workshops, and even festivals. Knowing that I am not alone, and being able to reach out to others who are further down the line than me for advice, makes a huge difference. Seeing milestones being reached daily on my feed, inspiring. Those who started on the same day as me are my online comrades in arms. It's truly eye-opening when you realise just how many perfectly 'normal' people have developed a dependency on alcohol, and we're just the tip of the iceberg, of that I'm certain. And you know what is comforting to realise? Your problem is not solely or specifically you. It's the drug called alcohol. Like some kind of omnipotent hypnotist, it creates the same pattern of behaviour and the same inner dialogue in all of us who have become dependent.

Alcohol, the socially acceptable, constantly encouraged, highly addictive drug is marketed to the hilt, hiding its truth in plain sight.

There is no doubt that all these distractions made it possible for me to move more recently into phase 3. However, I must just say one more thing about this critical phase 2 period. At any point I could easily have cracked and poured myself a drink, as so many of us do. It is a challenging time, but the more you overcome those challenges such as work do's, family events and big nights out (and discover that doing them sober is really not as bad as you imagined they would be) the more that mental muscle of yours builds itself up and hardens your resolve. Phase 2 is also a time full of exhilaration. The unbelievable energy coursing through you, the sheer relief of not waking up in the middle of the night soaked in regret and, instead, waking early in the morning with a surge of anticipation of the day ahead. Clarity. The childlike joy in response to the simplest pleasures that neither money nor booze can buy.

PHASE 3: ACCEPTANCE

I feel as if I have walked through a hidden door into a secret garden, the stormy, exhilarating weather I've encountered replaced by the gentle sounds of nature. So what about those uncomfortable feelings? Well, yes, they still come, but now something different is happening. I am not automatically looking for distractions to divert them. Instead I'm staying with those feelings, allowing them to pass

through me. I am recognising them for what they are—
feelings. And they're very important, these uncomfortable
feelings, because they are my subconscious trying to tell
me something. Sometimes, they are not even that: they're
simply my body giving me a nudge. "I want food, and I
mean food, not alcohol, okay?" it says to me.

If I feel bored, that doesn't mean I now have to have a beer
to lighten things up. I am bored. That is a feeling that
human beings have, and as frustrating as it might be, that's
life. So, now what can I find within myself rather than within
a bottle that will re-engage me? Or perhaps I could just
read. How grown-up is that? I am feeling tense and I am out
with friends in a bar. Well, that's okay. I am in a bright,
brash, noisy place, and frankly I'm a bit tired. That's
perfectly normal, particularly if I am not going to take a drug
I used to rely upon to manufacture feelings that are not real.
But look, I am with friends and I know the tension will pass.
They pass surprisingly quickly as I navigate my way into a
conversation and sip on my alcohol-free lager. Within an
hour I will be more present and more engaged than most of
the people around me because I won't be drinking. Then
another time the stronger and even more uncomfortable
feelings come: feelings which are perhaps based on some
unresolved experiences I have spent so many years
avoiding. That is good, because this time there is nowhere

to hide. So, I look at those feelings in the eyes, scrutinise them, ask them what they are trying to tell me. I start to make connections. It starts to make sense, why I am feeling what I am feeling. I can now make some choices. I can talk to someone about them, or work things out for myself and resolve to do something on my terms, which will help me to move on.

I am now dealing with reality and it is liberating because it is, as it says on the tin, real. As people who have stopped drinking often say, life suddenly appears in HD, warts and all, and it is quite something. The exhilaration of phase 2 just grows and grows here. However, I am under no illusion that temptation has gone, that I will not experience some very tough challenges in the future when it comes to alcohol. But something has changed now that I've moved into this place of acceptance.

No more fighting those feelings, no more trying to avoid them or having to distract myself. Just finally embracing a completely new reality full of feelings and wonder and truth.

Chapter 1

Magic Pyjamas

On September 6th, 2018, just four days after arriving in Sober Land, I discovered Magic Pyjamas. Actually, I discovered them in my hotel room, but the point is that I had suddenly found myself, already stressed and bewildered in this new reality, heading to the airport for a work trip to Frankfurt.

I wasn't ready. I really just wanted to be escorted to some Buddhist retreat which bans alcohol (actually, I'm assuming they do anyway) and not stumbling through an airport with my sober goggles on, completely spaced out. Not dragging myself into WH Smith or Boots to pick up some water and a thin sandwich rather than heading for those lovely champagne bars I used to get so excited about while I waited for my plane. Ah, I loved sipping a glass of cold, crisp wine and chomping into a prawn something-or-other, and then cheekily ordering another wine before heading for the plane, feeling all warm and squiffy.

Instead, I sat with the people I used to look at with a certain disdain. The boring people—holier than thou, I used to think—not consuming anything, just sitting and reading. Squashed into the boring seats in the boring areas dotted around the airport. All I could think of was alcohol, and the fact that I was sitting with the riffraff while the sophisticated, classy people sipped on their wines and champagne over there. It didn't occur to me at the time to question why they were doing so when it was only late morning or, for that matter, why the masses in the bar behind me were downing pints.

I just wanted to be with them—the fun people.

Next, I was on the plane: once one of my favourite drinking establishments, now a hell hole in the sky. *Yes, go on, person next to me, order two miniatures at the same time while I order two tomato juices with Worcester sauce.* To be fair, with Tabasco, the spiciness of the sauce helps a bit, but not as much as the magic pyjamas (which I will get back to). I remember sitting there, high above the clouds, thinking that if I stayed in Sober Land, life was going to simply be very flat, forever. Healthier but flat, all on one level, middling, no highs, no lows, a Groundhog Day of limited, repeated sensation.

When I reached my hotel, I was desperately thinking about my options and the possible distractions which would get me through the late afternoon and evening. I really wanted to meet up with my colleagues, but I knew that when we got together, sooner or later they would begin pouring ice-cold pints of lager down their throats as we discussed tomorrow's business. What the hell would I do? That's banned in Sober Land. So, there I would be sitting, uptight, taking pathetic sips of lemonade while they basked in boy's banter and alcohol-ignited, joyous anticipation of the evening ahead. I just couldn't face it, particularly as we would be having dinner with clients who I'd never met before while I was stone-cold sober, unable to smile without forcing myself, feeling empty, agitated, dull and with nothing to say. Ok, that's a bit dramatic, I realise this now, but that is where I'd got to with alcohol. It was the thing that lit my fire.

So, I checked in and went to my room, closed the door behind me, unpacked my bag and just stood there. Usually I'd be leaping around the room like that mad monkey in Hangover Part II, speedily hanging things up, putting things away, everything done with unbelievable efficiency and focus so that within two minutes I would be on my way down to the hotel bar. Instead I now moved like a depressed sloth from the bedroom to the bathroom, placing the contents from my wash bag, agonisingly slowly, one by one, next to the sink. As I shuffled back into the bedroom, I saw my pyjamas lying there in my bag. It was 5.30pm.

Surely, no, you can't put them on now for God's sake. You are a sophisticated communication skills expert on a work trip to Europe. You can't get into your pyjamas at this time while the rest of the world is pouring out of the workplace towards all those lovely bars. You sad, sad man.

But, yes, as if in some sort of a trance, I put those pyjamas on.

And then something amazing happened. I wanted a cup of tea. I didn't want a beer or a glass of wine, not really. Suddenly that overwhelming and agitating desire to have a drink became something more abstract and manageable. That's the power of association. I associated pyjamas with, for want of a better word, cosiness. Biscuit time. Getting ready for bed after having already had my fill of booze. What a discovery. For a moment I seriously wondered whether I might be able to wear my pyjamas AND go out. Could I get away with wearing my shoes and a jacket over my pyjamas and somehow look fashionable? Then I could join my colleagues, drink tea and smile smugly, pitying those poor souls who needed to drink to relax and enjoy themselves. Thankfully, I talked myself out of that idea and instead called one of my colleagues, told them I was unexpectedly exhausted, and ordered room service.

I had discovered Magic Pyjamas! Gloriously dull garments which would transform Clarke Kent-like into superheroes (both tops and bottoms) and come to my rescue time and again over the next few months.

The next day I bounded down to breakfast full of energy, an energy I can honestly say is one of the most beautiful side effects of sobriety. I delivered my part of the training course without a bead of sweat—sweating was always one of the most embarrassing side effects of having had too much alcohol the night before—rosy-cheeked, not pallid. Ironically, I probably behaved like that mad monkey throughout the day, but at least this time it was for the right reasons.

Adventures in Sober Land

Chapter 2

Christmas in Sober Land

Strap yourselves in, we're heading for the epicentre of Alcohol World—it's Christmas time! Traditionally this was when I would usually go berserk, yet here I was, three months in, living in Sober Land. Ah, Christmas, the ultimate homage to booze when it rolls out the red carpet, turns on all those sparkling lights and pops its cork for every guy (and girl) it sees. As we know, Sober Land is not a place but an inner world we project onto Alcohol World, and I can tell you this—when Christmas is in full swing, that projection is barely visible. You have to strain really hard to see it because there are no suitable backdrops or serene views. It's just a full-on razzle-dazzle of parties, work dos and supermarket aisles awash with booze. I found myself in a sea of alcohol, adrift on a little life raft made of alcohol-free beer cans, carrying a supply of tea bags, chewy sweets, and chocolate biscuits. And Magic Pyjamas.

In mid-December I attended a Christmas work do, arriving in the afternoon for the 'work' part of the day, where we would review the year just gone and look at plans for the next. In the past, I used to spend this bit politely nodding and smiling whilst listening eagerly for the first sign of the clinking of wine glasses being set up in the next room. When the first clink was heard a wonderful relaxed energy would begin to flow through me, and all of a sudden I would find myself enthusiastically contributing ideas, earnestly listening, and roaring with laughter at the 'in-jokes'. I knew that in thirty minutes or so festivities would begin and the work part of the day would be packed away. The anticipation was everything.

This time, I dreaded the idea of hearing the clinking glasses. The work part was like a warm, safe blanket to hide under and I didn't want it to be lifted. I remember, I actually enjoyed this bit and I contributed ideas thoughtfully, listened calmly and smiled—rather than roared—at the in-jokes. All too soon we moved into the next room for 'drinks and nibbles' with others' energies noticeably rising. Two colleagues, who'd already been out for lunchtime drinks, released themselves from the restraints I realised they'd had to strap on for the afternoon. That must have been hard work, being slightly squiffy while listening to annual projections. All I could think of was how early I could leave. I realise now that this was one of the many challenging situations which you just have to go through if you are going to live in Sober Land, and each test you pass makes you that much stronger. I searched amongst all the laid-on bottles of booze for some alcohol-free beer, but as always the only soft drinks on offer were orange juice and water. Because non-drinkers desperately look forward to those drinks at Christmas, don't they? I stayed for about ninety minutes, and when the first slurs emerged and conversation became circular, I made my excuses, wished everyone a fabulous Christmas and disappeared into the dark evening. As I walked Alcohol World's city streets, I remember thinking that something had started to change somewhere within me which might, just might, be the start of something permanent.

Which is just as well, because a week later a kind grotesque panto was about to start its Christmas run.

At this point, I think it's important to let you know that I have three children (aged fourteen, thirteen and nine at the time of writing this) who I live with and who were, therefore, present throughout Christmas. I don't intend to refer to them much in this chapter unless absolutely necessary, but they were there, *right* there, watching the panto. Indeed, it was precisely because they had watched so many of these kinds of 'shows' (in which I'd previously played a starring role) that I'd decided to stop drinking in the first place. I also want to point out that, from this point, my use of the terms *heavy drinkers* or *drinking heavily* in no way indicates that I believe said drinkers have a drinking problem unless I specifically say so. Which I won't. People change their drinking habits all the time, as some have in this case, but either way, I know, you know, we *all* know lots of people who drink heavily; it doesn't mean that they're an alcoholic, whatever that actually is. The bottom line is that I was a heavy drinker, and drinking heavily was the norm in my circle.

Anyway, it was now Christmas Eve and the heavy-drinking (see above) triumvirate of wife, mother, and mother in law had gathered. Only a year ago we had been a finely tuned, seriously well-oiled quartet of drinkers 'par excellence' but I had abandoned ship. I felt guilty. I remember pulling into my driveway with my crumbling mother in tow, whom I had picked up from her home a good three hours away. Driving through the darkening afternoon I'd sipped on cups of coffee while, in the passenger seat next to me, my mother would now and then twist open the cap of her water bottle, with her poor arthritic fingers, and gulp down a mouthful of warm, dry white wine. Not that heavy-drinking parents shape the future drinking habits of their offspring, or anything. The funny thing is, even then, I actually thought it was quite normal. After all, there had been times not so long ago when on long journeys home after work I'd stopped off at an M&S petrol station and picked up one of those miniature bottles of red wine and a vegetable samosa. With a napkin on my lap and samosa in hand, I would have myself a little 'mobile' picnic, washing down the spiciness with sips of red wine as I merrily made my way in the outside lane back from Norwich or somewhere like that. It somehow made me feel like I was already home. All snug. Bless my cotton socks, hey. I mean, it's one thing your mother of eighty-five years sitting next to you, guzzling white wine from a water bottle, but what about me driving, having a mildly boozy picnic? I convinced myself that I never actually drove over the limit when consuming one of these bottles as 187mls is the equivalent of just over a small, single glass of wine.

Of course, hearing this out loud sounds pretty feeble. Whichever way I look at it now, I can but hang my head in shame at this confession. For that reason, I resolved that in no way was I going to start preaching to anyone over Christmas.

Talking of Christmas, here are some of the highlights from the show.

My mother in her wheelchair—she can barely walk now and that's without the drink—nodding off at the kitchen table during mealtimes, having had too little to eat and too much to drink. She'd occasionally wake up, confused, talking repeatedly about her childhood in Africa, or her three failed marriages, before taking another slurp and nodding off. I wheeled her off at one point and left her in the sitting room because it was a bit of squeeze around the table when we were clearing the plates. I kept rushing in and out of the kitchen to check if she was stirring. Sometimes she was fast asleep but at other times she was surprisingly awake, just sitting there with her glass of wine, staring straight ahead. I knew, no matter how dazed, she would always find the glass which I had left on the table next to her.

My sozzled wife and mother in law, swaying panto-like, trying to help me leverage my mother into bed, while all three of them cried at various times or in unison during this military exercise because my mother was declaring, equally sozzled but horizontal, that this would be her last Christmas on earth—she could feel it in her bones. I couldn't actually feel her bones at all, which was what was worrying me.

My mother in law, wife, and mother all shouting at me at the same time, telling me I was a control freak. I think I was attempting desperately at the time to establish contact with Sober Land and therefore was showing real signs of strain. They must have interpreted this as a look of disdain regarding their vast consumption of alcohol. To be fair I might have been feeling disdain, at least to some degree, but most of all I was experiencing waves of desperation. I kept disappearing upstairs and connecting with other desperate strangers on our private alcohol-free Facebook group. That was a lifesaver, connecting with others on the same journey as me as well as the more experienced and serene sober gurus who guided me through my first sober Christmas in 2018.

Doing six fifteen-minute car trips to the local pub and back. Delivering one batch and then returning for the rest and then doing all that again for the return journey—all just to have our Christmas lunch out. Having to drop my mother and her wheelchair off along with my wife first, so there was someone with my mother in the pub, return, pick up my mother in law and my children, and head back to the pub. Eat lunch. Then do the same again in reverse. That's an hour and half of zipping about when we could have just taken two cars and done it all in one go for a total of 30 minutes. All because of one thing. Alcohol. However, it gave me a purpose and you really need that in Sober Land.

Waking up hangover-free on Christmas morning, having soberly laid stockings on my children's beds the night before, all with superb balance, complete focus and as silently as a lion edging towards its prey. The year before it was all quite different: nodding off on the sofa with a glass of red wine and huge chunks of cheese, waiting for my children to fall asleep upstairs. Then standing outside their rooms, listening for stirring, swaying, forgetting to breathe until I suddenly had to take huge gulps of air. Going back downstairs, having more red wine, but this time with some chocolate orange slices. Then going back upstairs, gathering up the stockings, which made the most horrendous crackling sound as I picked them up, and which I kept telling to be quiet as I made my way along the landing. The feeling that I was about to take on the most terrifying mission, the enemy all around me, as I mustered up the courage to enter the rooms of my children. Promptly losing my balance and trying to brace myself against the wall while frantically gripping the increasingly crackly stockings, which I continued to curse at under my breath. Clumsily laying the stockings on their beds, leaving their rooms, and taking in more huge gulps of air, having forgotten to breathe again. Finally, crashing into bed at about 2am, knowing that in only a few hours my children would be up nice and early to demand that I watch the opening of the stockings.

This time I was already up, feeling clear-headed and energised. A year ago, I was feeling dreadful. Hungover, grumpy and very, very tired. For that brief hour on

Christmas morning, Sober Land wiped the floor with Alcohol World.

Adventures in Sober Land

Chapter 3

Running Away

When I was in my mid-twenties, I decided I wanted to go travelling. You might want to replace that with "I decided I wanted to run away." I do wish Truman Capote in Breakfast at Tiffany's had been on the Piccadilly Line with me as I headed to Heathrow airport that day:

> *"You call yourself a free spirit, a "wild thing," and you're terrified somebody's gonna stick you in a cage. Well, baby, you're already in that cage. You built it yourself. And it's not bounded in the west by Tulip, Texas, or in the east by Somali-land. It's wherever you go. Because no matter where you run, you just end up running into yourself."*

Unfortunately, he wasn't available. However, my girlfriend at the time was. When I look back, I wish I had had the courage to bring it to an end there and then, because she deserved so much better than me. I was supposed to be going travelling, to explore the world and embark on a lifelong ambition to see more of this planet, all planned before we met. Instead, I went on one enormous drug binge in the Far East and Australia. As we said goodbye to each other in that airport, both crying, the previous twelve months flashed through my mind. The drug binge thing was kind of inevitable, looking back on it. I clearly suffered from mental health issues, yet at that point in my life I was unable to fully absorb this truth, let alone articulate it.

I knew I felt different to how I imagined other people around me felt: less in control, more erratic, more obsessional, more insecure, but I didn't know how to express this feeling. I simply lived it out in destructive and self-destructive ways and so it is not surprising, looking back at myself as I was then, that I gradually slipped into a pattern of self-medication. I'm not certain I'll ever be able to fully gauge how much my childhood events determined the state of my mental health, versus my natural disposition to feeling anxiety and depression. The countless divorces and upheavals, boarding school from an early age, an absent father, alcohol too present, and listening not present enough. And, dare I say it, all too often a feeling that love was conditional. These things clearly played a part, but I now fully recognise that I am simply a sensitive soul anyway. How very annoying.

So, there I was, twelve months before I set off on my travels, an out of work actor, working at the Palladium

Theatre in London front of house, a blue coat (and occasional red I have you know), completely wasting my time drifting on an ocean of booze and recreational drugs. Yet, growing amongst this wasteland, a few buds of potential appeared for a while before being overwhelmed. Having said that, I did have some memorable experiences.

For a start (and I can't believe I am committing this to pen and paper) I became 'the' Jason Donovan lookalike at the time. There, I've said it. And what made this the more extraordinary and sadder was that I happened to be working front of house in the very same theatre where he was starring in Joseph and His Amazing Technicolour Dreamcoat! So, there I was, tearing tickets, saying out loud but very quickly so people could not be sure I had said it: "Can I tear your nickers, please? Nickers please, tear your nickers please." Try it now, it sounds like tickets if you go at great speed and yet at the same time people are certain they have heard the word knickers. Oh, how we'd fall about in hysterics, me and my fellow blue coaters. I really knew how to use my time well in this, the prime of my life. I bathed, simultaneously, in reflected glory and deep shame when again and again the audience would think Jason Donovan had come out front of house. Not to say "can I tear your nickers, please"; of course that *would've* have created a stampede.

I would go along with the faulty identification, goaded on. Girls would swoon and giggle for a brief second then realise that it couldn't possibly be Jason they were seeing, because the genuine article must be getting ready to go on stage and earn thousands of pounds a show. So, with a final disdainful shriek, when they realised it was just me, they would be off to see the real thing. My complete lack of self-esteem momentarily lifted only to be dropped further down each time. I don't think it was very good for the soul, come to think of it. However, I did earn a few pounds from this sad deception, so I shouldn't be ungrateful. I appeared on Noel's House Party, did some strange dancing and singing thing live on TV in Brighton somewhere for Comic Relief, appeared on the front cover of Smash Hits, opened a seedy night club somewhere and danced with a girl at her bat mitzvah, when for about two minutes she thought she was actually dancing with Jason Donovan until she realised I didn't have a particular mole on my face I should have—at which point she started crying.

As Mr Donovan left the theatre through the stage door every evening to greet his adoring fans, I would sneak out that same door, amongst the shadows, with a bag of hash cakes and disappear into the evening with a friend or two. Doppelgängers heading in completely different directions.

Mind you, those hash cakes were something else and were sold to us by a very unassuming lady on the stage door. Ten pounds for a bag of ten—that's just one pound to get you completely stoned for the evening! I sometimes wonder if our Mr Donovan might have bought a few himself too. So it was at night that I would work as this blue coat, and occasionally as a red coat, where I would look after the VIPs with my friend Anthony (not his real name—it's not his fault I chose to write this ridiculous book) who is still my very good friend and wise counsel.

We used to serve the VIPs champagne and canapes at the interval and each time we went behind the screens and out of sight to collect more food or refill glasses, we would stuff our faces with vol-au-vents and down glasses of champagne in one. We'd re-emerge with canape-filled cheeks and the room starting to spin. To this day I am deeply concerned that a piece of asparagus might have been sticking out of my mouth when I served Princess Diana.

But what of my daytime routine? Well, in amongst the lookalike work and half-hearted attempts at auditions for shows, the recording of maudlin songs I had written, of inventing board games or obsessing over ideas for game shows (as well as regularly getting completely off my face) one of those 'buds' of potential I mentioned did emerge for a while before disappearing under the weight of too much weed.

I was on holiday in Majorca when I heard the news. Being completely hungover, I'd fallen asleep on the beach under the midday sun and woke with half my face completely red and the other completely white, a perfect line between the two running down over my forehead, nose, and chin. Jason Donovan, eat your heart out. A call came through from Glyn, my mentor at the time and BBC radio producer, and with the hotel reception beckoning me, I zigzagged my way, dehydrated and confused, off the beach to take the call. The BBC had commissioned my dramatisation of the Adventures of Tintin for radio! That was it—I would never have to do lookalike work again because I was about to hit the big time.

I would be bigger than Donovan himself and would go on to write a film version of The Adventures of Tintin with Steven Spielberg—come to think of it, why didn't he ask me? After all, we went on to win a Bronze Sony award, a second series was commissioned, and I even continued this Hollywood-like success by adapting Gulliver's Travels for radio, too. Actually, Radio 3.

I was only young, so sitting in a studio in Broadcasting
House with the likes of Andrew Sachs (playing Snowy the
dog of course) Miriam Margolyes, Leo McKern, Lionel
Jeffries, and Stephen Moore was somewhat overwhelming.
They were actually reading and recording *my* adaptations. I
used to walk out backwards from rooms, ever so slightly
bowed, as if in the presence of royalty, such was my sense
of unworthiness. I remember I used to wail with laughter at
everything they said and would wholeheartedly agree with
every suggestion they made to enhance the production.
"Absolutely. Fantastic idea. That's brilliant."

But life is all about the choices we make. My troubled mind
and desperate need to avoid my feelings pointed me away
from my current path, which felt too smooth and manicured
to possibly be true. So, I headed off into the undergrowth,
where I felt more comfortable and suited to be, and made
my way, beer in one hand, spliff in the other and some sort
of tablet on my tongue. It was time to travel the world and
leave all notions of possible success behind me. The
beauty of running away was that I would never have to
know if I would have failed or not.

I was heading for Australia to see my older sister Jenny and
family there, but my first port of call was Bangkok. Funny
how I just happened to choose that as my little two-day

stopover, wasn't it? Now, at this time, Anthony (remember him? My wise counsel?) was also travelling around southeast Asia, but he was doing it properly. We had arranged that we would meet in Australia at some point in the next few months, but, for now, it was time to venture forth alone. Exciting. Whilst I knew he would still be having fun, of course, I also knew he would be visiting, for example, those extraordinary temples and historic sights of that country, linking up with fellow travellers and staying for a day or two on its beautiful beaches and talking way into the night under the stars. Staying with local families throughout his travels across Thailand, Indonesia, and other neighbouring countries, learning their customs and taking in the different cultures of all the places he visited.

I, on the other hand, would not.

No, when I arrived in Bangkok, I headed straight to my hotel, did the two-minute unpacking thing (even then) and headed off to the enticing bars I'd heard all about. I was up and running, heading full-on into a blur of ping pong balls flying at me from every angle and from the most eye-watering of places—girls, beers, vodka shots, the lot spilling all over me and a man at one point cracking my neck while I was going to the loo. Extraordinary, he just came up behind me, got hold of my head, and quickly twisted it. I had to hold on for dear life to ensure that I was still pointing in the right direction, but I must say my neck and shoulders felt wonderfully relaxed after that. I think I was supposed to tip him, but I wasn't sure where that would lead.

I do remember meeting this English guy who was completely wild. He showed me around Bangkok in a series of Tuk Tuks, travelling from bar to bar. We got completely drunk and I recall ending up in a very upmarket hotel restaurant, dressed inappropriately, sat at a piano. I think I had told this guy I wrote songs and he insisted I play something. I just remember this insane face looking at me, but as he was very large and imposing, I felt I had to oblige. So, I started to sing quite possibly one of the most depressing songs I had ever written. As people chatted, sipped on expensive wine and ate their lovely food, I was singing "Father don't make me cry again, what do I do with all this pain." After three songs, of varying levels of self-indulgence, I actually received applause. However, now I look back on it, I think this was their collective way of saying, "Okay that's enough, you sad little man trying to sound like some weird blend of Elton John and George Michael but doing both really badly. Oh, and why are you impersonating a completely wasted Jason Donovan?"

I landed in Sydney two days later, feeling culturally uplifted. I hadn't seen my sister for several years and I was very excited about seeing her and my nephew, as well as other members of my mother's family, including my aunt and grandparents. This is where my mother had lived for many years, and this is where she had run away *from* when she was in her twenties to come to the UK. This was also where my sister had run *to*, from the UK, to find her long lost father—not mine, hers, though she regarded mine as hers, which sounds complicated but isn't really. Funny, that. The running away thing must run in our family.

As I exited departures, I saw my sister charging towards me, so very thin and small and manic—and very light as I lifted her almost above my head by mistake. It was lovely to see Jenny, but I couldn't work out why she had lost so much weight or why her eyes were so big and wild.

The next few months were a blur of hedonism. I knew something wasn't quite right when, at about 6am on day one, I came down the stairs of my sister's house and she was standing on a chair in the kitchen, in her clothes from the night before, doing the dusting. I thought she was incredibly house proud and had a very strong work ethic. I was quite impressed, but still, I couldn't work out why she was so thin. On day two, she disappeared into her bedroom and didn't come out for about sixteen hours. She'd had nothing to eat since I had arrived but I noticed now, as she emerged, that she was scurrying up and down the stairs, taking with her tray after tray of food and drink. Sandwiches, crisps, chocolates and quite a bit of champagne. Fascinating, I thought, as I sat there getting stoned on some quite extraordinary grass she'd given me from a bag in a cupboard which seemed full to the brim of the stuff. My nephew of sixteen sat with me, rolling joints with frightening expertise. I wish I had said something then, had done something about this crazy situation I suddenly found myself in. No judgement. No blame. Simply, this should not have been. But I was too self-absorbed, too weak and too dependent myself to do anything. And I am truly sorry for this.

On day three, we were about to go out for the evening to eat in the restaurant of the Sydney Tower. My sister's boyfriend was joining us, along with a good friend of hers. My sister asked me if I'd ever had the 'champagne' drug. I said indeed I had, and very often when serving VIP's as a red coat. They all laughed and my sister said she could no longer keep this from me. With that, she opened a cupboard door. There was quite a lot of white stuff in what seemed like hundreds of little bags and I was taken by how neatly packaged it all was. I remember that night, arriving at the Sydney Tower, wanting to talk forever and eat absolutely nothing that was in front of me, which was a bit annoying at first. I kept doing this strange thing with my mouth and noticed that no matter how much champagne I drank it seemed to have absolutely zero effect. I thought I was magnificent, and that I could change the world with these extraordinary thoughts that were racing through my mind.

This need to continue talking went on when I was lying in bed and suddenly noticed my sister's friend had joined me, completely naked. She had slipped under the covers and had climbed on top of me. Unfortunately (and probably rather stupidly, now I look back on it), I kept getting out of the bed, sitting on a very large cushion in the corner of the room, and wanting to tell her all about a new game I had just invented. Or about why I was starting to believe in reincarnation.

Day after day, my sister would give me pocket money, a couple of spliffs and a little bag of the white stuff and I would venture off into Sydney to do some 'sightseeing'. She seemed to have loads of money. Days turned into weeks, a kaleidoscope of people, parties and endless nights spent somewhere a long way out from my head.

Then something happened. I remember a gun being wielded by someone visiting the house one night, and I insisted we leave immediately. So, we were off, heading north to my sister's rainforest, which she had bought recently. It was an extraordinary place, a thousand acres of quite stunning land and trees. My sister was an amazing person who'd ended up in a bad place in her life. Not the forest, of course, that was beautiful, but within herself, for all sorts of reasons I won't go into now. And so had I. That's the irony. A brother and a sister desperately trying to escape their feelings but unable, for some reason, to articulate this. At least, for that brief time, we had each other. But before I left there was one last trip my sister insisted I go on, and she promised she would be by my side all the way.

So, as I sat there in trepidation, waiting for takeoff in the middle of this stunning rainforest, my sister handed me two lovely looking little LSD tabs. They were quite cute, as it happened, so I placed them on my tongue and allowed them to dissolve. Then I started to catastrophise. *What happens if I never come back? This just isn't the kind of thing a neurotic with low self-esteem should be doing right now!* But my sister held my hand and took me out onto the veranda of the lodge we were in, and just told me to take in my surroundings. She was a mischievous thing, she really was. Talk about introducing her little brother to new experiences—she was about to blow my mind.

The first thing that struck me was how utterly stunning and vivid the colours of the forest became. My God, I was in paradise. I was amazed at how large the flowers of the forest were growing, rising above my head as I made way down to the stream on top of what appeared to be giant petals. The frogs were talking to me and I was sure I saw Snowy, the dog, run past me with Andrew Sach's head on his shoulders. I was standing in the middle of the forest and able to direct the sound of the cicadas. I could welcome the cacophony in its full glory, or channel it so it only came at me from one direction, or amazingly, with a swish of my arms, I could wipe out the sound altogether. Next I was running down a track in nothing more than a pair of pants and some quite sturdy boots and happened upon a Kangaroo, who bounced over my head. That is actually true; I am certain I didn't hallucinate that. Then later I stripped completely and climbed up a tree next to the lodge. My sister failed to tell me friends of hers were coming over. As they walked up the path they all looked up at me and my sister said: "Oh that's my brother, by the way." Can you imagine what greeted them, looking at me, stark bollock naked, from below? I was simply trying to make my way up into the Milky Way and wanted to be left alone.

A week later I left and headed home to the UK and into the arms of my girlfriend once more. I had not travelled the world; I had travelled out of my mind and I was spent. So, I hauled on my blue coat once more, cut my hair as Mr. Donovan cut his, climbed on board my little boozy boat and set sail once more towards my late twenties.

Adventures in Sober Land

Chapter 4

The Dinner Party

When you arrive in Sober Land and hand over your passport, a clean fresh page is turned and the stamp is pressed firmly into the centre of it. The previous pages, crammed with all the stamp marks of your countless stays in Alcohol World, are now out of sight. Those stamps represent the roaring, heady, tumultuous times spent with friends, going out (or staying in) and getting, well, drunk. And those times are now gone forever. That thought hit me hard as I walked through arrivals and out into the bright and glaring light of my new Sober Land home. I would never again get drunk with any of those friends, ever, ever again.

Help! I want to go back. I didn't mean to buy a one-way ticket. It's all been a terrible mistake!

Please, I'll will pay anything, I shouted, trying to bribe myself. But it was too late. I'd spent the last ten years knowing I drank too much and had endured so many failed attempts at stopping that, like some young (ok, middle-aged) man embarking on a trip around the world in their gap year, I knew this time I had to go. If not now, never.

45

This time I was not running away, I was running to. Despite the pain of leaving behind loved ones and the fear of being alone and entering the unknown, there would be no turning back.

It was like a bereavement in some ways, and the saddest thing was, it was for the saddest of reasons. Alcohol had become my best friend. A friend who had, in many respects, taken me away from my real friends. Ironic, then, that I now felt so sad at leaving them once again. At least that's how it felt at the time. I now realise that my life had shrunk in on itself and I had begun to occupy a very small space which consisted of being at home, albeit with my family, every night—except when away working—rarely doing anything else but consuming a bottle of wine every evening in the kitchen or sitting room. Finish work, drink, feed children, drink, monitor homework, eat, drink again, sleep. Very busy doing the same thing again and again. Time spent with friends, my true friends? Negligible. Yes, dinner parties occasionally, and always organised by my wife. Now and then a boys' night out. Staying with a mate occasionally when away working, that kind of thing. But I had lost the drive to contact my really good friends and plan proper get-togethers, weekends away, activities. To make an effort.

I lost contact with some people I should not have lost contact with. Yes, I was busy, I had a young family and maybe I am beating myself up a little too much, and maybe they could have contacted me more often too, but at the heart of it all, my disconnection was down to my drinking. Alcohol was enough. It took up my time and my attention. I was able to withdraw into my bubble, potter around, do a bit of this and that with a glass of wine or beer by my side to keep me company.

Anyway, before I completely disappear up my own backside, let's change gear here by comparing and contrasting the joyous act of going to a dinner party, both in Alcohol World and in Sober Land.

***

We're going to a dinner party tonight and it's still three hours until our taxi arrives. I've already had a couple of beers at lunchtime with my cheese and onion sandwich (I love that combo) because, well, it's a Saturday and it would be rude not to. I am having a bit of debate with myself. If I have a glass of red wine now, then that should be okay because later I can have a cup of coffee to offset the inevitable drowsiness which will follow—my mother likes to call it a siesta—or I could have a couple of red wines, but have them out of a small glass rather than the large glass I have just reached for. What do you think? Right, I've decided. I am going to go for two small glasses because that will take me up to 5pm, when I can still get the coffee in. The large glass will probably mean a 4.40 pm finish and that leaves a little too much time, I think. After coffee, I can then take the dog for a walk to freshen up (me, not him) before having a gin and tonic to pep me up ready for the taxi and the evening ahead. Great! Meanwhile, I've noticed my wife has continued with the white wine since lunch. But since it's been gentle sips rather than giant glugs, fingers crossed it doesn't catch up with her later over dinner.

The babysitter arrives twenty minutes before takeoff. I'm quite perky on the back of that G&T. It hadn't worked initially and I was really worried I would turn up at our friends all drowsy, which would be a nightmare. I hate that feeling. My wife is quite perky too, but I'm concerned that I might be ever-so-slightly slurring in the same way she is as we both desperately overcompensate by being all brisk and efficient. I wonder what my children think, too; they've seen us in our respective bubbles this afternoon, showing little engagement and purpose, yet all of a sudden we're full of enthusiasm with the babysitter. We give our children lots of kisses as the taxi pulls in, and for some reason, I suddenly feel like a fraud. Anyway, I smile, tickle them, put on a silly voice and then we're gone.

We arrive at our friends' place and I'm quite excited because she cooks the most fantastic food and he makes the most amazing cocktails. They are the perfect hosts. We enter the kitchen and I wonder if they too have been drinking through the afternoon. Normal people don't do that, so they can't have, but something inside me hopes they have, just so I don't feel like some freak. I mean, they certainly like their drink so why wouldn't they also have a problem, as I have? Or do normal people reserve getting blotto for Friday and Saturday evenings only?

The first cocktail is delicious, but then it is always is. We have an earnest conversation about its various blends and fusions and how it gives just the perfect kick at the end. I spot various bottles of red around the kitchen, plenty of white in the rack and one chilling on the table. I am both relaxed and fired up at the same time. We will not run out, that's for sure. Right now is the perfect part of the evening. There's a warm glow around us all, I feel, as we talk about our children, work, holidays, memories of previous inebriated evenings and the ridiculous things that happened or were said. My wife and I are wildly enthusiastic about the food being served and then we all proceed to out-compliment each other about the lovely food each serves at their dinner parties. We even go into detail about the particular starters, main courses and puddings consumed, how they were made, and make grave promises to exchange recipes. As always, I hold my hands up saying that I have absolutely no idea how to make cocktails, so there is no doubt I lose hands down in that category.

As the evening goes on, I'm pretty sure we're talking about the same things as before, but there are always two new juicy pieces of gossip that form the centre piece of discussion. One from us and one from them. We return to these stories several times throughout the evening because when you're high it's particularly thrilling to relive their outcomes. It somehow makes you feel very good about yourselves when you discuss the demise of the central characters being discussed.

Brandy and coffee are taken in the sitting room at around midnight with a taxi half an hour away. I am really quite drunk now but I never actually lose control, of course. However, the reason I know I'm drunk is because my quips have been replaced by droning philosophy. Also, I can actually hear myself slurring specific words (like the word specific) fairly significantly, which I find really irritating. However, that's nothing compared to what I suddenly notice on the sofa opposite me. The white wine my wife consumed in the afternoon has caught up with her and she is now laid out, fast asleep, snoring. I've only just noticed this but now I realise why our friends were trying not to laugh when I was dismissing the existence of God. I then immediately proceed to call upon God when it hits me that I'm going to have to get my wife into the taxi.

The next moment I'm zigzagging towards the taxi with my wife over my shoulder. I then spend the entire journey home profusely apologising to the taxi driver before disembarking and zigzagging once again towards our house, where I pause, my wife still over my shoulder, and pay the babysitter. Finally, after a couple of three-sixty turns as I try to get my bearings, I make my way up the stairs, one strained lift of the leg at a time—as if doing some seriously hard resistance work in the gym with some even more seriously heavy weights—before unceremoniously dumping my wife on the bed. Note: my wife is not that heavy, but she appears to be when I'm drunk.

I wander downstairs incredulously, having checked on my sleeping children and thanking God (who I don't believe in) that they are blissfully unaware of all of this. I go to the kitchen cupboard, find a large wine glass and drain the remaining red wine from the afternoon's open bottle into it. I even snap off a good-sized piece of cheese and spend the next forty-five minutes at the kitchen table straining to read posts on my Facebook feed, sipping, nibbling, completely lost in a meaningless blur of other people's lives. Finally, after the eighth or ninth violent nod of my nodding-off head, I ascend the stairs to bed, already knowing that I will be feeling dreadful, once again, in just a few hours.

***

We're going to a dinner party tonight and it's still three hours until we need to be there. I've already had an alcohol-free lager at lunchtime with my cheese and onion sandwich (I love that combo), because, well, it's a Saturday and it would be rude not to. I am having a bit of debate with myself. Shall I go to the gym or just go for a quick run? Or shall I just have one of my mother's siestas?

Problem is, I'm not tired. In fact, I've got too much energy. Right, I've decided, I'm going to go to the gym, because that will take me up to 5pm, when I can still take the dog for a walk to freshen up (him not me) before having yet another cup of tea. Damn, I am seriously addicted to that stuff. Meanwhile my wife has continued with the white since lunch, but it's been gentle sips rather than giant glugs, so fingers crossed it doesn't catch up with her later over dinner. In around eight months she'll have begun her own journey into sobriety, but right now there's a real clash between Sober Land and Alcohol World here in our house. It's tense and I need to get to the gym.

The babysitter arrives twenty minutes before takeoff. No panic (since I'm driving) but I do hate being late for things, so it's good to see her. I'm quite perky on the back of that gym session and my wife is quite perky too, in a completely different way, and I can tell she is desperately overcompensating in front of the babysitter. I am so hyper-aware now of the effects of alcohol and I feel my stress levels rising whenever I sense she has reached the tipping point. I wonder what my children think too. Now that I'm sober, I can see when they're annoyed at any signs of inebriation in the family. Interesting, that.

I wonder if they have seen us in our respective bubbles this afternoon: me in Sober Land and her in Alcohol World. Nevertheless, I have consciously spent time with them today, playing football with my son earlier, planning with him to go ten pin bowling tomorrow, and trying to have a chat about 'stuff' with my teenage daughters. How embarrassing that must have been for them, me asking them who their favourite artists are, and yakking about the fact I like that Norwegian singer, Siegfried or whatever her name is (you mean Sigrid, Daddy!) but hey, I tried. I have been far more present for them since I stopped drinking and I hope that has registered. I also hope they know how much I love them even if I do sometimes get a bit grumpy dealing with my new life and what is happening in our home of clashing worlds. Before heading for the car, I give each of my children a single, heartfelt kiss. It is such a relief to feel there is no need for pretence, for feeling that I am somehow being deceptive.

We arrive at our friends' place and I am quite excited because she cooks the most fantastic food and a bit stressed because he makes the most amazing cocktails. Tonight will be a test, but I have already been through some major tests and the truth is that it's only when we put ourselves in these situations and find a way through, unscathed, that our sober resilience actually grows. The point is that Sober Land exists inside Alcohol World, not outside it, so, guess what—you just have to get on with it. The thing I'm dreading most is breaking the news that I am not drinking. That, and just flagging at around 10pm.

We enter the kitchen, and I wonder—have they been drinking through the afternoon? Something inside me hopes they haven't, just so I don't feel like some freak. I mean, they certainly like their drink but in no way does that mean they have a problem. When it comes to drinking, I don't know where you draw the line between normal and abnormal, between people reserving it for Friday and Saturday evenings to get blotto, or people gently topping themselves up throughout the week. I used to do both.

I announce, as soon as I can, that I am not drinking tonight (forever, actually, but sshhh that will completely ruin the evening) as I withdraw four bottles of alcohol-free lager from a bag. I tell them I have a really important conference call with a client tomorrow at 6am, who is flying over from China later in the day. And that's why I drove. Yes, I know, a conference call on a Sunday. Yes, I'm furious, but there's nothing I can do about it, I continue to protest. That last bit sounds a tad forced and I'm sure they're not entirely convinced. I look across at my wife, who, on the journey here, was told to back me up as I didn't want to have to explain at this stage that I have chosen to no longer drink.

But she looks at me, perplexed. "A conference call?" she says, somewhat disgusted. "What do you mean, a conference call? It's Sunday. You don't have a conference call, that's ridiculous." *Oh God, she's completely forgotten.* "Simon's decided not to drink anymore, but he didn't want to tell you."

Oh, dear Lord, this is a bloody nightmare. For a split second, I consider jumping into my car and going on a very long road trip across America.

"Oh yes," my wife suddenly says, remembering. There's been a break in the clouds and she has recalled the story she was supposed to go along with. "Yes, he does have a conference call. An annoying client of his... flying over from America."

Our hostess tactfully changes the subject and asks my wife how her mother is. Meanwhile, our host smiles at me and asks if I have really given up drinking. "If so, hats off to you because I don't know if I could."

Wow, I wasn't expecting that. I really wish I hadn't mentioned the conference call thing. That's going to induce one of those sudden involuntary face-cringes which strike from nowhere, now and again, for the rest of your life. "Oh, I don't know," I bluster, "Just trying to get a bit fitter, need to lose some weight, I'll probably be back on it next weekend." I desperately want to reintroduce the conference call thing to see if I can convince him that it's true, but then reconsider. No, I'll just pretend it was never said.

"Fancy a mocktail?" my friend asks.

The first mocktail is delicious, but then it is always is. We have an earnest conversation about its various blends and fusions and how it gives just the perfect kick at the end. I spot various bottles of red around the kitchen, plenty of white in the rack and one chilling on the table. I am surprisingly relaxed, something I have noticed more and more recently when spending time with friends who are drinking when I am not. The first ten minutes or so are always a bit tense while I adjust to the fact that my state of mind will not change much that night, that I will not experience the loosening of the tongue, the fuzziness of the brain. It's still all relatively new to me, this calm and present state.

Much of the evening runs as it has before, talking about children, work, holidays and even memories of inebriated evenings and the ridiculous things that happened or were said. It's even funnier recalling those things sober because I am watching people (drunk) recalling those things. Yes, watching drunk people talking about times when they were drunk is hysterical, because it's as if they've completely forgotten they are drunk. A bit like someone very old and decrepit mocking someone who is very old and decrepit. Or a very young child telling you about the childish things they did when they were very young.

Brandy and coffee are taken in the sitting room at around midnight. I can't believe I'm still awake; I'd intended to leave at 11pm latest. I am of course drinking a mint tea because that is what I do now, for God's sake. What's slightly disturbing is that it dawns on me that droning philosophy is just what I do at this time of night anyway, and has nothing to do with drinking. We really must leave before I bore our hosts into a coma. Also, there's the small matter of the white wine my wife consumed in the afternoon; it's caught up with her and now she's now laid out fast asleep, snoring. I noticed this some time ago, as did my friends, and we have been laughing rather hysterically at the huge and sudden snorts which emanate now and then from the sofa, and which keep making us jump.

The next moment I am walking in a straight line, extremely quickly, towards my car, with my wife over my shoulder. I have spent the last ten minutes profusely apologising to our friends, but they're well away and just can't stop laughing. The journey home is silent, bar those huge and sudden snorts. I wind down my window and allow the sounds of the air to take over. I love this sound, travelling through the darkness, sober, listening to the rushing night. Being able to just get into a car and drive anywhere at any time is one of the most unexpected joys of sobriety. It is a symbol of the complete freedom you gain from no longer being dependent on something which used to dictate your every move.

I leave my wife in the car while I go into our house to pay the babysitter. It wouldn't be fair on her or my wife to walk in with a body hanging over my shoulder. Once the sitter's gone I collect my wife, who is also completely gone, and I carry her up to the bedroom. I have to admit I still enjoy the 'dumping on the bed' process.

I wander downstairs, having checked on my sleeping children, thanking God (who I still don't believe in) that they are blissfully unaware of all of this. I go to the kitchen cupboard, find two large mugs and make two steaming cups of tea. I take one up to my wife, along with a pint of water for the gasping reach which will come in the early hours, and go back downstairs. Yes, I still scour my Facebook feed, but this time within the private Club Soda group. Nice to connect with like-minded people at this time of night, who've successfully navigated a boozy evening of their own.

I can't say I feel truly comfortable at this very moment because right now Sober Land and Alcohol World are, well, worlds apart. One thing though, I just love Sunday mornings now. They are the ultimate reward for abstinence. So, with that thought, I head for bed, calm, clear and excited for tomorrow.

Chapter 5

Holidays

Ah, going on holiday. What a wonderful thing it is. Perhaps its greatest thrill is in the anticipation, in the planning, in the discussing of it. In the imagining of it, in having the light in the distance to be heading towards throughout the winter, in the bookings of restaurants and activities and the announcing that "this time next week we'll be in X." And, at the heart of it all, the knowledge that you will have guiltless permission to drink to your heart's content from late morning to the evening if you so wish. Nothing more perfect than going on holiday with both your best friend and your family.

And, just like with the work trips, the airports and the planes are all part of the indulgence. As is heading straight for the local supermarket after landing to get supplies in (despite the children's protests) even though the villa is closer. The unpacking, the checking out of the pool, the deciding who has which bedroom—none of this can be done without a beer or G&T being sipped.

I remember during my drinking days, when I tried to envisage life without alcohol, the thought of 'dry' holidays was the deal-breaker and I would simply reach for my glass and bury my head once again. I would often say to myself that there would, in fact, be no point in ever going on holiday again if I stopped drinking. So, when you really do remove the booze and take that first trip, the prospect is quite overwhelming. I can only liken it to how I imagine a child would feel at the thought of Christmas with no stocking, no presents, no chocolates, and no Wi-Fi.

So, if I may, I would like to show you some snaps of holidays both before and after the seismic decision to stop drinking. I hope you enjoy flicking through the album that is this chapter.

***

We're in the south of France with the children, my mother in law and her sister. We have rented a lovely villa with a pool; a beautiful veranda overlooks the sun-baked lawns and a large table occupies the cool shadows under the grapevines, where their fermented cousins are being poured generously, as always, from midday. It's great. The children are playing in the pool or playing cards with granny, aunty, and mummy while daddy works on some game he is inventing, or something he is writing, staying in his little bubble, moving between lager and red wine while the ladies are on sparkly or crisp dry white. I do of course plunge into the pool to play with the children now and then but, truth be told, as much to freshen up a bit as to spend quality time with them.

It's mid-morning on day three and we're already disproportionately worried that we're running a bit low on the booze. There is, of course, still enough food to last about four months. No one wants to be put in the uncomfortable position of even having to remotely think about the prospect of rationing certain drinks. There has to be a sense of endless abundance in that department: the knowledge that one could nonchalantly open yet another bottle of vino and yet, right there before you, stand a thousand more. The problem is that we won't have a hire car until week two of the holiday (when the mother-in-law and aunt leave) and the villa is about two miles from the nearest small town. Yes, I could call for a taxi, but I fancy a manly adventure into the unknown. Or, to put it another way, the nearest supermarché. If I am being honest, I'm feeling a little delicate—hungover with a vaguely troubled tummy.

No matter, I will do what has to be done.

I bid farewell to the family, with my rucksack on my back, the only man in the group, my role to forage, to hunt and gather as many bottles of Sauvignon blanc, sparkly, full-bodied red and lagers as I can carry, and drag them back to the cave.

I set off wearing a t-shirt, a pair of bright blue trunks (see later) and trainers. After about a hundred metres, I feel the vivid heat immerse me. Blimey, it's hot and dry out here on the road. Intense too with the sound of crickets, a kind of teeming silence which oppresses. No matter, I will not turn back. I like this feeling of being alone in the wilderness with the regular passing of holidaymakers in hire cars and taxis, thundering lorries and local people going about their business on mopeds, bicycles or in dusty vans. I begin to wonder when I will see the first signs of life; the road feels so long and hot and I'm starting to feel a bit dodgy. At last, in the distance, I see an avenue of trees that marks the beginning of the small town and I feel a real sense of release.

Unfortunately, so does my stomach.

I try to ignore this feeling and focus on the trees in the distance and the beautiful shade they look to offer. About two hundred metres out, approaching a bridge that serves as a kind of announcement to the avenue and town beyond, I feel the need to gently break wind. Just the merest release is all that would be required. Silent and without troubling anyone. But instead, in a moment of clarity, I ensnare it with a mighty clench of the buttocks, stopping in my tracks to ensure all energy and focus can be sustained and also because I'm concerned that the mechanics of a walking bottom might unleash hell. Thank God the clench works. This is what heavy drinking does, you see—it plays havoc with your digestive system.

I reach the shaded avenue and feel a sudden, overwhelming sense of accomplishment as if I have made base camp and can now take stock of the next part of the mission from a position of relative safety. I also feel much better stomach-wise, as if the clenching not only trapped but also completely eradicated the windy menace. I contemplate doing a little jig but can see people walking towards me in the distance. Life is good, life is exciting. I now turn my attention to the map on my phone to ascertain where I am and which way to turn next to reach my destination, just fifteen minutes away.

Then it happens again: that feeling of something needing to escape. At first I'm calm, assuring myself that I'll be able to apply another mighty clench if need be, then make my way smoothly to a nearby cafe—there has to be one, surely!—in order to deliver the killer blow in the privacy of a toilette. However, something feels a little different this time, something more persistent, urgent, with an unmistakable need for self-expression. Yet at this point, it really does just feel like another requirement to 'trump', no more no less.

So, I stand looking up the long, straight avenue, spying the approach of those people who were in the distance, but who are now much closer. I pretend I'm admiring the beautiful architecture and how the speckled sunlight through the leaves casts hypnotic shapes on their exteriors—which of course do not register with me at all, a man trapped in a brain in full 'flight' mode. The good news is that those people are still an inaudible distance away and so, with that reassurance, I begin preparations for release. I do so in a way I have discovered many times before works, mitigating any concern about sound or indeed velocity. I do this by very carefully, very discreetly pulling one cheek (no more than a centimetre I'd say) away from the other.

Unfortunately, this backfires.

Yes, it sounds like wind, it feels like wind, has the subtle air of wind. But it is not wind. I realise, too late, that on this occasion, the separating of the cheeks only serves to encourage rather than nullify. For a brief moment, when the deed is done, it does feel like I have merely trumped, admittedly at greater length than is usual. I tell myself that I really do need to stop catastrophising.

I allow the people to pass, shouting "Bonjour" with a giant, manic smile. Next, still hopeful, I reach my right hand round beneath my rucksack and down to my bottom while looking ahead, smiling at the gloriousness of my surroundings. My hand reaches its destination and what it discovers, quite simply, is not dry land.

Oh dear God, no, please no.

Not here, in a small town where I know not what waits beyond the avenue I am on, what lies north, south, east or west. Perhaps my pants have saved me, I say to myself, in that perhaps that extra layer will mean that little evidence will be displayed.

Then I remember. I'm not wearing pants because I am not wearing shorts, which I'd assumed I was. I'm wearing *trunks*. Why the hell am I wearing trunks? A thin, stretchy light-blue material is all that separates a giant 'shart' from the world! In the excitement of embarking on this safari, I'd forgotten to change. I desperately try to calm myself. I even tell myself—as if in an out-of-body experience, which is actually a little too accurate—that one day I will look back at all this and it will give me endless chuckles. However, that doesn't work one little bit.

I look around, saying to myself that if I want, I can stay here forever, right here near the bridge overlooking that river and in the shade of these trees. A river! Yes, that's it, I can jump off the bridge and plunge into the river! I am wearing trunks—it was meant to be. But wait, it's very far down and I have no idea how I would get out, and I would draw huge crowds. Then I spot a front garden with a large hose in it on the other side of the road. More people are now approaching, and from both sides, but if I do it confidently— simply march over there, climb over the small fence, find the tap somewhere attached to the house, turn it on, make my way to the centre of the garden, and stand there hosing my bum—that will be okay, won't it?

But I realise that both ideas are completely idiotic. There is no way out. I have no choice. I must simply now walk. Walk until I find a café. And when I find that cafe I must simply find a way of reaching a toilette, without anyone noticing the catastrophe in my trunks, either on the journey there or in the last moments as I enter the building. I then must make my way to the toilette, the location of which I will not know until I'm in there. Oh, God. That means I will have to ask someone, and in the asking I will be found out. I will have stopped too long to try to find the words in French, which I can't speak, and as I ask the waiter or waitress, locals rich and poor will gather to see the terrible truth from all sides.

I am catastrophising again.

Calm down.

So, I begin to walk. As I do so, I come up with what I think is an ingenious plan. My rucksack, short as it is, could be my ticket out of this. I just need to find a way to use it to cover the terrible mistake. I realise that taking my rucksack off and simply holding it against my buttocks will not only look ridiculous but will draw significant curiosity. Yet the rucksack is too short to naturally cover my rear while still strapped to my back, stopping a good three inches above what would have been my belt line, had I had been wearing something that required a belt.

My solution, as I stood there, this human blemish staining a picture post card view of a Provençal avenue…

It didn't exactly cover me with glory (and let's face it, I had little enough glory to spread around as it was), but here it is.

I proceeded to walk with my shoulders pushed back as far as they could go, back arched significantly, as if preparing to look straight up at the sky, but with my head and eyes fixed, instead, straight ahead of me, creating a sponge of double chins. Surely this contortion would lower the rucksack over the disaster. Alas, as I reached down once again, I realised I was still an inch off. Weaving through the throngs like Basil Fawlty at the height of desperation, I kept telling myself that perhaps a shadow might be cast by this 'act of lowering', a dark cloud cast over a murky patch of field on a bright summer's day.

I reached the end of the avenue where it suddenly dissolved into a busy main road, cutting straight across me left to right. It was all so much bigger and busier than I'd ever anticipated. I was so overwhelmed I had a sense that I was completely naked, which would in some ways have been preferable. Being naked but clean in the middle of this town in the South of France would have brought comfort in comparison to what I had become, this foul and stinking shart-stained Englishman. Oh God, I'd allowed myself to forget about that. It was a painful and almost paralysing reminder that I must have stank, too.

Then I spotted a café on the other side of the road. People were gathering behind me, waiting to cross. I cannot tell you how long it felt before the lights on the pedestrian crossing changed; it truly was a living nightmare. I expected someone behind me at any moment to scream out in horror at suddenly spotting the giant imposter in my trunks. I'm talking about the one at the back—there was nothing giant round the front, I can tell you. Like the rest of me, it just wanted to run away and hide. A frozen prawn hidden at the bottom of a bag. The lights changed and I leaped across the road, now taking enormous strides because I'd got to the point where frankly I didn't care anymore.

The entrance to the café was not directly off the street but instead through a strange little garden, lying parallel to the road, with a small path running up the middle of it to a glass door. There were tables and chairs either side of the path and, yes, people were sitting at them. Another kind of avenue now, this time made up of people drinking coffees or early beers and delicately nibbling on pastries. Could this be one giant prank, where friends had: set me up on some fly-on-the-wall TV programme, having planted exploding sharts in my trunks set off at just the right time to cause maximum impact; created a route packed with crowds pushing me onwards to a busy main road; arranged an

71

excruciating delay at the pedestrian crossing; and, finally this, the ultimate feat, provided a cafe with a purpose-built walk of shame?

I started to edge forward. As I did so, I remember thinking that the people facing me as I approached would not be a direct threat. It was the ones with their backs to me who were about to become the real problem. I hated them already as if they had purposely positioned themselves that way in order to espy the terribleness in the back of my trunks. They would then nudge their friends and I would be transported into some grotesque catwalk scenario. Me, this sad little 'everyday man' modelling a new line in 'farty' pants with ready-made stains, created bespoke for pathetic little men who find that kind of thing funny.

I will never know how many of those people saw the evidence of my awful accident, and frankly I don't want to know. All that mattered was that I reach that glass door and find the bloody loo. A waitress with her back to me was talking to a couple near the door, blocking my path. I stopped, then hesitantly and quietly squeaked a "Bonjour." She didn't respond and so I just stood there with my back to the human avenue. "Excusez Moi," I continued to squeak. A flicker of response could be detected in her shoulders, but it was clear that she knew a grovelling Englishman stood

behind her and she would not be rushed. I decided it was
better to retain my bottom's current direction, facing both
downwind and down the human avenue I'd already passed.
At least the eyes back there would have had their fill
already. This way I would not have to introduce the
spectacle to anyone new, including the waitress.

So, feet firmly planted, I stretched my head around the side
of her face from the back, giraffe-like, and said very loudly
"Toilette?" She looked at me briefly and gestured that it was
just inside the glass door on the right. I could see a look of
complete contempt in her eyes, even from the side. With
my face still there, I said to her cheek, in a very strong
French accent, "I will have coffee afterwards," because I
wanted her to know that my visit to the loo was of mild
consequence and my real reason for entering her
establishment was to enjoy the fabulous food and drink.
With that, I charged forward, shoved the door open (almost
shattering it), looked to my right, and… joy! There it was,
and it wasn't occupied!

What came next was quite possibly the most fantastic
fifteen minutes that I have ever experienced. Just me, in a
small bathroom, with a sink and a loo, splashing and
scrubbing in a furious celebration of freedom. My meagre
and somewhat smelly surroundings were to me as beautiful

as the most expensive hotel suite I'd ever stayed in. At one point I was completely naked, quite possibly just for the sake of it. Apologies, I wasn't intending to show you that particular holiday snap. The only downer, apart from that image, was having to squeeze on those trunks again, wet and clinging to my thighs as I dragged them up to their rightful place. Again, apologies. Anyway, they were clean!

I was feeling that little jig coming on as I opened the bathroom door to exit, but then I suddenly realised I was re-entering the scene of the crime where onlookers would be gathered, waiting. Waiting in anticipation at what they would see emerge, and this time the press would have been alerted. I took a deep breath, pulled on a smile, and stepped out. But no one batted an eyelid. I did for a moment feel like I might be Truman Burbank, the Jim Carrey character in The Truman Show, where he doesn't realise he's on 24-hour TV or that everyone around him is a cast member. The moment he enters somewhere, or steps out, everyone is 'on' and the performance around him starts up. Was this happening to me? Then I wondered if I was still actually hungover and had entered the paranoia phase.

I decided I needed to play them all at their own game, to call their bluff so that people might even start to question whether they'd really seen the horrific sight that had made its way through the garden and into this establishment. Instead of fleeing, I went to the bar, almost sticking my rear outwards, so confident was I in its newfound squeaky-clean status. Then, instead of thinking clearly, recognising why this had all happened—a combination of alcohol flooding followed by acute dehydration—what did I do? No, I didn't order a long glass of ice-cold water or perhaps a cup of tea.

I ordered a long glass of ice-cold beer.

You see, that is what dependency does. It has no regard for you. For your body or your mind. It's so clever that it doesn't even let you consider it until much later, after the event, usually around 3am. That's when the despair of what you're doing to yourself strikes, when you're alone in the dark, sweating, regretting, promising yourself that tomorrow you will not drink. That you can't go on like this, that if you do you'll probably die and leave the most terrible legacy for your children, who you love with all your heart.

But right then, I took a sip, let out a quiet sigh and determined to find a little table to sit down and lose myself at for a while. I stepped into the garden, where of course no one looked up, and found that little table, next to a low wall which ran along the side of the pavement I had recently leapt along. I took out my phone and searched the map for the supermarché. It was about seven minutes' walk away. It was by then 11.45am and I wondered whether I would or would not tell the family back in the cave (where I would soon be dragging the bottles I was about to capture) of this particular adventure.

***

We're crossing the arrivals lounge at Dubai airport, full of excitement at what lies ahead at the beginning of our week away. My wife is either some way back or some way ahead of us, depending on the ebb and flow of energy that a plane journey full of wine and fitful sleep brings: one moment a surge of manic endeavour, and the next a deep desire just to lie down. I remember that feeling very well and so it's a relief now to be both naturally tired and naturally excited on this, my first sober holiday. The children are equally tired and excited, so things could go either way.

I'd been to Dubai several times before on work but this was my first time holidaying here and I was experiencing mixed emotions. On the one hand, we would be guaranteed sunshine, brilliant accommodation, restaurants, service and a sense of opulence, as well as a vast pool in our hotel's exotic, manicured gardens and thrilling water parks. On the other hand, I knew it wouldn't be a particularly cultural and rustic experience, nor entirely relaxing when we stepped out of the confines of our place of stay. Dubai is a land of huge contradiction and irony, where laws are strict and your freedoms clipped and yet behind the walls of plush hotels the very things banned are indulged to the maximum. Which is a thought made further poignant by the fact that we'd decided to take our holiday here in Dubai during Ramadan. The idea to go at this time had appealed to me for two reasons. One, our hotel was, as a consequence, half the price it would have normally been. Two, I wouldn't be the only one sacrificing something!

Anyway, I loved the idea of seeing Dubai for the first time completely sober, on holiday, and through the eyes of my children. Even the plane journey had felt so different, sitting there next to my young son, watching films, playing games, reading, chatting, occasionally nodding off together, with his face pressed against my arm, drooling. Being in the moment, even when inside a long tube in the sky, was great, instead of the desperate need to punctuate the experience with booze. The constant looking around and getting fretful at not being able to have another red wine 'right now' because cabin crew was otherwise occupied. Measuring the journey by the glass. Pepping myself up with coffee and then cutting loose and slowly drifting away from myself with wine, back and forth.

We exited arrivals into a dry and enveloping heat, a very different heat from my infamous walk to that town in the south of France nearly two years before, and this time there was no chance of igniting that terrible 'Lehman's-like' collapse of my large intestine. No danger because I was two stone lighter (almost all due to no longer drinking alcohol), immeasurably fitter and healthier, with a sphincter operating according to the user's manual. However, I have to admit I was getting stressed by my wife's unpredictable state, and I kept saying under my breath, when I saw a wave of irritation or impatience cross her face, "Remember we are in Dubai."

I recognise this was probably a controlling act, but this is what can happen when one of you makes the choice to stop drinking and the other one doesn't because they haven't reached that stage yet, and you are married to each other. Me irritating her with my controlling anxiety, and her irritating me with her alcohol-skewed responses.

I really enjoyed the taxi ride to the hotel because I was able to watch my children's responses to seeing things for the first time. However, I almost certainly infuriated them by continuously pointing out landmarks and recalling memories of my time "in that luxury hotel over there", or "that massive building where I worked", all to prove what a cool, jet-setting dad I was. Finally, much to their relief, we reached the hotel. Weirdly, I love that mixed feeling of awe and anticipation of looking up at the stunning exterior of the hotel where you'll be staying, versus the dread that it might all be a façade for a huge disappointment within. I know, that's not normal, is it? Perhaps I have a gambler's nature and it will turn out to be my next addiction.

The people who greeted us on the door were ridiculously welcoming and respectful. In a way it was almost too much because I kept feeling I had to return the same level of commitment to happiness and warmth. It was as if I was being drawn into a battle of animated facial expressions, hand gestures, and beaming smiles. And it was also very hot now.

Entering the air-conditioned and unfathomably opulent entrance to the hotel was a joy, the cool air hitting us like a beautiful greeting all of its own. We checked in, got the lift up, and raced down the corridor to a large door that signalled the entrance to our room. Inside was more opulence and four beds were strung out in a row for us all to choose from. The bathroom was very large and there was ample space for a family of five to stay for a week— and I mean *inside* the bathroom. Stepping onto the balcony, we could see the exotic gardens and abundant pool below, and beyond the trees a glimpse of beach and sea. In drinking times, I would have been scouring the minibar and room service menu to work out my booze bearings along with accompanying prices. Right now, I just wanted to grab the children and my trunks (which were not bright blue) and head on down. Which I did. Meanwhile, my wife said that she would unpack our bags and then just chill out for a while.

I do love not knowing where everything is yet, the restaurants, the best areas for maximum shade, even the best ways of getting in the pool. I enjoy being a newbie because it means you still have the whole holiday ahead of you. This hotel was so grand that people were employed to stand by each exit into the gardens and greet you with an enormous smile and gracious bow—which of course I returned every time, with an even bigger smile and an even lower and more gracious bow. If only I could behave like I saw some others do, being aloof, proud, giving barely anything back to these greetings save the faintest, barely detectable raising of an eyebrow or twitch of the mouth. A little crumb of sustenance for the grateful souls who were honoured just to be there in the first place. Souls who'd travelled on dreams from desperately poor countries to find a way of earning money to send back to their expectant families. Families they saw perhaps once or twice a year: children, husbands, wives and parents reliant on this one person who had sacrificed themselves to provide for their loved ones.

So, you see, I couldn't do the aloof thing. I remember thinking that my little gesture at giving up alcohol and the struggle to do so was embarrassingly unimportant compared to what these people had given up and struggled with. Most of us have no idea, do we, what it means to live the lives of people who take these hugely courageous and often painfully lonely steps?

Feeling somewhat like royalty, my children and I made our way out into the exotic gardens and headed for the pool, stopping on the way to pick up towels and bottles of ice-cold water from one of several 'stalls' dotted around so people didn't have to walk too far, poor things. It was 40c and that *is* hot, but because it was a dry heat, it was manageable so long as there was a pool to plunge into. At around midday there were barely any sunbeds available, so we dumped the towels on the single one we could find and hurried to the edge of the pool.

There's something very different about entering a pool on holiday, in the heat of the day, without a drop of alcohol inside you, compared to the experience of doing so after a few beers or wines. I can't work out if it's psychological or physiological, but when the water hits your skin sober you feel so much more alive. The experience of pushing through the water or ducking beneath the surface is natural and vibrant; you feel entirely connected to what you're immersed in. When weighed down with booze and feeling drowsy or a bit squiffy, it's all a bit of an effort, a bit of a shock to the senses, a means to an end—which for me was primarily to wake myself up a bit. For some reason, whenever I did something active or exerting after a few drinks, it felt like I'd put on something which was far too tight for me. Two contradicting states coming together.

It was so good to be able to spend my days that week full of energy, completely alert yet completely relaxed. Enjoying just mucking about in the pool with my children, playing hide and seek in it; there were lots of faux pillars and plush ornaments to hide behind, though the sight of a middle-aged man taking it all very seriously, in little trunks, peering around giant vases, mouth open and 'desperate' not to be spotted must have been rather unsettling. It was idyllic: the chatting, the reading and the remembering of everything I read, the sleeping deeply and the joy of endless rides at the water park. Being able to take in a view of the sea or the city at night, and being at peace as I looked on. Peace, because there were no underlying feelings of guilt, nor was there any sense of something not being entirely right.

I still wonder how my wife was feeling. She said at the time she enjoyed the holiday, which is great, but I also know that she expended a significant amount of energy (and a ridiculous amount of money) ensuring she was topped up throughout the day and evening. The hotel charged an eye-watering £50 for the cheapest bottle of the stuff. They seriously have you by the spicy meatballs, behind those serene walls.

Revenge is always best served cold, ice-cold in a beautiful glass. Watching my wife's inner battle between getting her fix and regretting the worth she had to put on it was difficult, but I could entirely relate to her struggle. I understood that feeling very well. I'm sure there were many people on that holiday, around the pool, at the beach bar and in the restaurants, who were caught in this same dilemma from about 11.30am onwards every day.

I did wonder, in a moment of devilish fantasy, what would happen if I could get access to the Tannoy, cut across all that mood music in the hotel and throughout the exotic gardens, and announce:

"I'm terribly sorry to disturb you all, but just to say that, with immediate effect, alcohol will no longer be served here or across the whole of Dubai. Apparently, it's a Muslim country, it's Ramadan, and your gracious hosts at this hotel have decided it's time to commit."

[LONG PAUSE WHILE PEOPLE SIT THERE IN COMPLETE SHOCK OR START RUNNING FOR THE EXITS, IGNORING ALL THOSE BOWS AND SMILES, AND GET PACKING FOR AN EARLY FLIGHT HOME]

"Only joking. Fill your boots and have a great day!"

Chapter 6

Visiting Mother

(CUE MUSIC) I'm off to see my mother, the wonderful mother of wine, because, because, because, because.... she appears to be having it all the time.

God, I can't believe I just wrote that. Mum, I honestly don't mean to be rude, I just find making light of something fairly profound seems to help. I know you love your wine, and that's ok. It's your choice, and as you say, it gives you something to look forward to each day.

It's a good three-hour drive down to Wiltshire. I make this journey to see my mother now about six times a year, which I recognise isn't often enough. I have to say it's never an easy experience staying over, but there are always plenty of classic comedy moments nevertheless. Indeed, it was only a couple of months ago that I drove my mother home after her performance in the stunning black comedy 'Nightmare on Christmas Street', which I've previously described. We're still at that stage where the light of late afternoon fades fast, but something in the air is turning. I love this time of year, with Spring soon to break and

85

renewal around the corner. I was feeling a sense of renewal myself, but I would never be able to describe that feeling meaningfully to my mother because to try to do so might only appear to be making a point.

I pull into the car park of the warden-assisted complex of apartments where my mother lives. I take a deep breath, enter the block, and head for the little distillery along the corridor at the end. I buzz the buzzer and wait for the silence to finally break with a tiny voice saying, "I'm coming," followed by the sound of a Zimmer frame quietly, eternally moving over carpet. Finally the door is unlocked and then I hear my mother start to reverse the Zimmer frame; for some reason, I can't help picturing a very old goat retreating from a fence as one reaches out a hand. "You can open it now, I'm clear." So, I open it, but very carefully, because I'm paranoid that I will send her flying into the airing cupboard.

I squeeze in through the door and my mother is already travelling towards the sitting room. Not through the air of course but leaning forward on her Zimmer frame, unable to turn her head to greet me, set purposefully on course for her big, soft armchair—in many ways her second home. She reaches her destination and now slowly turns, like a small boat fighting against the tide, until she is in position to inspect me. She even puts on her glasses, one hand maintaining her balance on the handle of her Zimmer frame, to get a really good look.

I wait with bated breath for approval.

"You've lost weight again, Simon," she says, and I think that's a compliment. Once again, she asks if I am still not drinking, to which I reply I am indeed still not, to which she asks if I feel better as a result, to which I reply I most definitely do, to which she says that perhaps she should but actually why should she, because she's eighty-seven ("or whatever I am") and she wouldn't have anything to look forward to if she stopped. I remind her that she's eighty-five, but yes, I do understand. Probably not much point.

What I want to tell her is how sad I feel that there is nothing else for her to look forward to but drinking wine, that it's the only thing that gives her pleasure. That she cannot find that creative flame within her, or some passion or interest to absorb her. I want to ask her if it has occurred to her that the reason she lacks any real interest in anything meaningful is probably due to decades of wine consumption. That she still might have time before it completely extinguishes those things that could be stimulating her mind or, at the least, the possibility of them being able to do so.

Instead, I pick up the empty wine glass on the tray of her Zimmer frame—fantastic contraption that it is, enabling my mother to travel around the house with a glass of wine permanently to hand—go into the kitchen, and call out, "More wine, Mum?"

"Oh, yes please, why not," she replies, a little burst of laughter flashing through her voice.

Fast forward to later in the evening. It's dark and I am pushing my mother along the streets of Salisbury at great speed in her wheelchair, zigzagging between street-lit puddles, which prove a brilliant obstacle course on this the pre-dinner mini pub crawl. My mother's white hair is standing up on end like the wisps of a dandelion and I do get concerned that it's suddenly going to blow away. I think we're both experiencing a sudden feeling of freedom and I realise that this is my mother's passion. Not wheelchair racing, but the thrill of being out—of adventure. In the past, I would have accidentally steered the wheels into some of these puddles—can you be had for drunk wheelchair driving?—and the water would have sprayed up over her, causing either a cry of consternation or a wail of hysterics, but now, like an F1 driver, I clip the edges with precision.

I would've been starting to feel the first waves of relaxation at this point, knowing my friend 'Beer 'n' Wine' and I would be able to have a giggle later while my mother increasingly spoke in every decreasing circles. That was what was great about drinking on these visits; it always felt like there were three of us, rather than two, wherever we ventured. Now it was just me and mum, and I knew I had to seize this moment because it would only get more challenging later.

It's now about 7.30pm and I'm steering my mother into the French bistro we always go to whenever I am down. She loves it here, loves the thrill of being out on the tiles. I know where this all stems from, and I know where I too caught the bug. We lived in Majorca when I was a child, ex-pats in the beautiful town of Pollensa in the north of the island, and it was a heady life. Artists, writers, composers (my dad), the rich and retired, the rich and not retired all coming together in a spicy gazpacho soup of late nights in restaurants, bars and afterwards the 'Placa' (the town square) where the adults would sit outside the cafés lining its edges, getting plastered while children roamed and darted across it well past midnight. It is so indelibly stamped, within me and my mother, the association of warm evenings and cold wine, hers enacted and mine, at the time, observed, that even here on a late winter's night in the southwest of England, it could still be felt. As a child, I must have absorbed so many sights and rituals around drinking and its connection with having fun that it was almost inevitable that I would take up the practice. I imagine this must be the case for so many of us who develop a taste for it. On all the many visits back to Pollensa as a teenager, and into middle age, drinking has always remained the central theme.

I have wedged my mother under the lip of the table in her wheelchair and her Sauvignon is on the way, so I think we have successfully dropped anchor. She is again asking me if I have really given up drinking as if it's the most extraordinary act to have ever taken place. Which, thinking about it, it probably is. If only she knew how hard it has been and how dependent I had become. But I can't bring myself to tell her. In doing so, the spotlight would inevitably swing round and rest on her, and the light would just be too bright and too probing and would serve no purpose at this late stage. The rest of the meal is like sitting at one of those tables which you can spin to access different dishes, but instead of dishes, we revolve topics; three or four them keep coming around repeatedly and are explored as if for the first time each time, using the same questions and receiving the same answers. In amongst this madness, I switch my nodding head to auto-response and engage my mind elsewhere, taking in my surroundings. The first thing I like to do is spot the non-drinkers. When I see a table full of them, I'm intrigued. People actually choosing not to drink on a night out, not because they have a problem with it (I am assuming) but because they can either take it or leave it, or simply leave it. Non-drinkers are a rare species, here in the western world, and it's important, when you spot one (or even better, a colony) to record their behaviour. They appear to be having fun, but are not overt in their actions. There is something grounded, relaxed and natural about them and amongst the smiles, the occasional surge of heartfelt laughter comes as if to say, yes, sober people can end up in hysterics too.

How extraordinary it is, people not needing to ingest streams of booze directly into their brain on a night out, being accepting of their feelings, in whatever guise they happen to come, without the need to enhance or submerge them. I have had to learn the hard way to do this, like a fish that has somehow made itself onto dry land (because it was getting just a bit too dangerous in that there sea with all them there sharks) and which has managed to wiggle its way, in the nick of time, into a freshwater pool where the clarity is both extraordinary and disconcerting.

What about the energy I'm picking up from other tables in the restaurant? It's different. Still relaxed but less predictable. Manic, edgy outbursts of laughter or slightly dreamy gazes which could turn at any moment, one senses. People finding the sparkle of alcohol irresistible. I can't help thinking how mildly disturbing it is that so many of us have this need for to manufacture altered states of being in order to enjoy life.

Talking of altered states of being: "Simon, I think I might have to go to the loo." My mother has been picking at her steak and salad with her knotted fingers because a knife just doesn't, well, cut it anymore. In fact, I've been doing the cutting of the meat and she the washing down of it, apart from the odd choking fit which (I always think at the time) is about to mark the end of it all.

So, this is it, the moment has arrived. I'm going to have to escort the orangutan to the loo. *An orangutan?* you ask. *That's not very nice.*

I will explain. Whenever I have to help my mother across a bar or restaurant without the use of her wheelchair, it feels as if I am holding the hand of a small orangutan. This is not because my mother has particularly hairy arms or indeed any noticeable clumps of scraggy red hair, but due to two physical adaptions she applies to the process of walking. One, the rocking motion she assumes as she attempts to gain some traction moving forward. Second, the angle of her arm, slightly bent, as she holds it high above her head so my hand can guide hers. We can't use the wheelchair here in the French bistro because there are about six steps up between us and the loo. No, we have no choice but to make this trip on foot

Anyway, the point I'm trying to make is that my mother knows I call her an orangutan because I often tell her this as we make these trips, primarily to make her laugh. I find that a good chuckle gives her a little more speed both up the steps and along the long straights.

I carefully disengage my mother's wheelchair from under the lip of the table so that I can turn it outwards, ready for disembarkation. The footrests are pushed to one side to allow exit from the seat, up and out, but this is a fairly delicate part of the operation. I have to stand directly in front and request she raises both arms while planting her feet as firmly as possible on the floor. It does take a few practice hoists, but finally—and with a fair amount of groaning—she creaks up onto her feet. Phase one complete.

Next, we make a small turn on the spot, which is trickier than one might think. This is a centimetre by centimetre operation until we are pointed in the right direction. Then we're off. After about two minutes of high-intensity trekking, we've managed to cover about ten feet, arriving safely at the foot of the six steps. The orangutan's hand grips mine ferociously as we ascend and I take the full weight of this seven stone beast, who quite understandably lets out a few rich words of prognostication about how we'll never make it to the summit. However, finally, we do, and I now see before us the vast plains of the restaurant that we must cross, dotted with tables of people who have yet to look up and behold the splendid creature which has risen from the depths of the lower floor. We're heading for the disabled loos, which rather shatters my illusion of being on a safari. As we pass tables, occasionally someone does look up. If they are a kindly soul, sensitive to what lies beyond their immediate area of concern, they catch my eye and smile. Sometimes, it seems, almost knowingly.

Most people are well and truly locked into their conversations but a few, just a few, look up and directly through us. How can they not notice a tipsy orangutan is being taken for a stroll through the restaurant? Perhaps they have far greater beasts in their lives to worry about. Finally, we make it to our destination and I go to open the door to the great loo beyond. The one for the disabled folk, yonder. I open the door onto a bright and sanitised space, and on the far side lies the toilet and sink. They seem almost menacing. I escort the orangutan to these cold and callous ornaments, carefully turning her so she is once again facing the right direction for the purpose in hand. And then I tell her, as if I'm telling her I will never see her again, that I must now leave her and wait outside. She puts up a protest for a brief moment but then realises that she really would much prefer I do just that. So, as if I've just pulled out a block from a giant Jenga tower and am willing it to stay intact, I run across the floor of the loo and out through the door, closing it quickly behind me. All I can do now is pray.

I look around the restaurant from my new vantage point and try to picture myself in thirty years, being escorted across this same room by one of my children. Will I too have become an orangutan? Or will I have taken the form of, say, an old warthog, perhaps capable of trotting ahead of them but still needing instruction? Perhaps sturdier from a life lived without alcohol from this point on, but nevertheless gnarled and hairy. I hope I turn out to be a warthog because that would mean I'd have given myself a fighting chance of my children still wanting to be in my company, feeling that they could talk to me (albeit in warthog) and, perhaps, respecting me.

"I'm finished," comes my mother's voice.

I really do hope this means that she's now upright with dress in place. I open the door as if entering some dark cave that conceals something horrific deep within. My mother is standing there, holding onto the sink and waiting to be collected. Did she actually go to the loo or simply imagine she did? Has she been standing there all this time and has only just suddenly come to? Oh well, I guess we'll find out soon enough.

"That's brilliant, Mum," I say as I walk over to her. And with that, we make our way back to camp.

We're now in her little apartment again. I'd pulled into the side of the car park to allow enough space to be able to unclip my mother, hoist her out of the passenger seat, and drop her into her unfolded wheelchair. For a minute I had had to leave her on her own, there in the darkness and the gently falling rain, while I parked up properly. I looked at her through the car window, sat there all alone in her wheelchair, this little person silhouetted against the half-lit night. So very vulnerable. I wondered what she was thinking as she breathed in the elements, elements she probably wouldn't feel again until I was next down to see her.

"I couldn't have a nightcap, could I Simon?"

I go to the kitchen and open the fridge. There is one bottle of white half-full and another yet to be opened but ready to go. God, she's getting a bit low. I check the boxes in the corner and discover two more bottles waiting to be transferred for cooling soon. Phew. It's Wednesday and her next delivery will be on Saturday, which I will be ordering on Friday morning as I do every week. I try to make sure I always do this for arrival on Saturday so I have a sense of where she will be on the booze front on any day of the week when I'm not there. I always order her eight bottles of white and a litre of sherry for her weekly consumption along with various ready meals and the usual basics. In some ways, I feel like a kindly dealer. Or maybe not so kind?

I step back into the sitting room and see that my mother is resting back in her chair with her eyes closed. I quietly place her glass of wine on the table in front of her. She wakes immediately as if she's caught the scent of the grape passing downwards from on high. She's like a finely tuned truffle hog trained to locate and extract the fruit bodies of a Sauvignon blanc. Eyes fully open and suddenly alert, she asks me if I would like a glass, then remembers I don't drink, then once again tells me how amazed she is and what strong will power I have, and that there is no point in her giving up at her age. The truth is that I don't have any will power, that's why I can't drink, but I just smile and ask if she would like to get ready for bed because she looks tired and I'm tired too, and it would be good for us both to get a decent night's sleep. I say this very calmly and slowly to try to hypnotise her into a state of ready acceptance, because I'm getting a bit desperate now. Desperate because I'm going to have to also help her to bed, and I don't want her to end up in a horizontal position as she was last Christmas when everyone was crying and she was announcing it would be her last on earth and I couldn't feel her bones.

Eventually I place a glass of water on the bedside table next to her 'two-sips-short' of an empty glass of wine, which she will insist is not removed. I quietly leave the apartment and then tomorrow morning I will return to guide her to her armchair before the carer comes into to help shower and dress her. I will make a cup of tea for her, hand her yesterday's Daily Mail, and say that I must be on my way. She will not want me to go but I will tell her I will be down again soon, which might not be that soon because I live some way away and I am ridiculously busy.

Simon Eastwood

Finally, after checking she has everything she needs and promising her that her order will be with her on Saturday, I will make my way to the front door, looking back once to see her still sitting in her armchair. She will be listening out for the door to close because she is unable to turn to watch me go. I will feel a huge surge of sadness as I step out into the cold winter morning. I will close my eyes and draw in the icy air and promise myself that when I grow old I will be a warthog and not an orangutan.

Adventures in Sober Land

Chapter 7

The Festival

I have been to three organised 'sober' socials over the last year and all of them have been both affirming and somewhat surreal. These are organised by Club Soda, the mindful drinking movement I'm a member of, which I refer to in the introduction. I am going to talk more about the brilliant Club Soda in a later chapter, so, for now, I mention them just for context.

It was these sober socials that made me originally think about writing a screenplay about Sober Land; they throw up so much material for a classic British comedy-drama, like Four Weddings and Funeral, for example. The characters, the situations, the dialogue, the courage that sits behind the laughter of strangers coming together sober in the kinds of places where they used to get completely trashed. The reason I ended up deciding to write a book instead of a screenplay was simply that I've grown to realise that sometimes it's best to follow the path of least resistance, particularly when it's highly unlikely anything I write will actually get published.

I'm still working on my self-esteem.

The first event I went to was the Mindful Drinking Festival which took place one Sunday in London in mid-January 2019, four months into my sobriety. Sober Land was completely in its element that day, superimposed on every nut and bolt, every person, every conversation. Ablaze in wondrous, technicolour sobriety.

I had boarded the train bound for London the evening before, feeling like some lone hero, embarking on a perilous journey deep into uncharted territory. I would love to say I emerged from a thick, dark fog, appearing on the platform with the ice-cold air clinging to my rugged beard. But it was actually quite mild and I had just cut myself shaving before leaving the house, which was really very annoying.

On the train I fantasised about checking into some dodgy motel, lit up by a single blue neon light, along some forgotten highway, far from anywhere. Instead, I checked into a Premier Inn quite near Covent Garden. After unpacking my bag, neither with the speed of the mad monkey nor at the pace of the depressed sloth, I headed out. By this stage, four months in, I was starting to get into my alcohol-free beers, so my first mission was to find a place to eat, here in the heart of the capital, which served a

range of interesting alcohol-free lagers, spirits or wines. I
set off into the evening, actually quite excited.

But with each enquiry, which I delivered with an
awkwardness which rather alarmed me ("Oh, hello, I was
wondering if you served alcohol free lagers or wines by any
chance?") I received shakes of the head accompanied
either by completely blank expressions or with suspicious
looks of the 'what a weirdo' variety. Wow, was it such a
strange thing to ask? Perhaps it was. One thing was for
sure; I was seriously taken aback at just how many
restaurants did not cater *at all* for the non-drinker who still
wanted to have a 'grown-up' drink. It put into stark contrast
the place I'd be visiting tomorrow, with the mind-boggling
range of fantastic alcohol-free beverages that would be on
display. Finally, I found a bar which happened to serve food
and which had the one alcohol-free lager on the menu, the
good old 'Becks Blue'. I don't mind a Becks Blue at all but it
always feels like the 'we better stock an AF beer'
afterthought.

I sat there in the bar, and to be honest I was ok. There in
the heart of Alcohol World, I watched, Attenborough-like, as
people went about their social interactions. Couples at
tables, in deep or flirtatious conversation or sitting in
silence, comfortable or deeply uncomfortable, I couldn't

quite tell. Groups of men, groups of women and a mix of both, all bound by one constant and fundamental common denominator. And it wasn't food or sex—they would come later. For now, it was all about the booze. Booze served in seductive bottles or spilling over pint glasses, fizzing away in tumblers or dressed up in long, exotic glasses. I was struck by how many guises ethanol came in. Different tastes and strengths but all doing exactly the same thing. Getting people drunk. I felt a rush of envy, followed by a deeply sad feeling of something lost as I watched a young couple engrossed in each other, him pouring the final drops from their shared bottle of red into both their glasses, then re-engaging with her, both high, glowing, their lives distilled into that moment.

I left the bar and headed back to the hotel. As I walked through Covent Garden, lit up with pockets of people braving the winter evening, cigarettes and drinks in hand, I thought about that couple and how I, too, had been in that same situation on numerous occasions. High on life, love and lust, all fuelled by that same dreamy drug.

I got to my room and lay on my bed, in the dark, still fully clothed, and then it hit me. It was the bloody booze. That's what I was feeling so deeply sad and sentimental about. It was nothing to do with hankering after long-lost romance, or the overwhelming joy of being completely connected to someone—although that would have been nice. Booze simply blurs the experience of those things. They are infinitely more powerful and real without it. No, what I was getting all maudlin about was no longer being able to feel that blinking lovely squiffy feeling.

I arrived at around nine the following morning at the very cool Truman Brewery on Brick Lane for the Mindful Drinking Festival. I began to wonder why I'd volunteered to help at something I had never attended before when my role was to look after people who had never attended before. I made my way to the welcoming area and busily started moving around in circles, pretending to be preparing for something. Finally, Laura Willoughby, co-founder of Club Soda, came up to me and gave me a big hug. We had never met before, so that was nice of her. She made me feel very welcome and briefly explained that all I had to do was just make conversation with people who might feel a bit lost and show them generally where things were. She then proceeded to show me where things were because I was clearly a bit lost.

Laura made a good point that some people might turn up feeling pretty fragile. It made me wonder. Did I feel fragile, myself? I was so good at feeling something and then immediately dismissing it that I'm still not sure. Maybe not fragile, on reflection, but perhaps conspicuous. Ironic that there, in the heart of Sober Land, I should feel conspicuous. Perhaps I felt like I was about to enter the company of seasoned 'soberites' and I would somehow be found out. "Four months, you say. Ha Ha, I did four months five thousand times before I properly gave up."

But of course, everyone was lovely and normal. One person (already over a year sober) said to me that one day something inside you clicks and you just know. I think she's right. It was really good to finally meet people who felt the same way as I did, who'd found themselves in the same place with alcohol and who were doing what they had to do to change their lives for the better.

About an hour or so in, a good friend of mine, who I'd invited along because I knew she was also trying the not-drinking thing, turned up. Together we started to peruse the plethora of stalls displaying their no- and low-alcohol beers, wines and spirits. Most were extremely good. I thought yes, you guys are onto something here. You're all going to be millionaires within five years because the world will have discovered the terrible truth about alcohol and I, the lone hero, will have been the catalyst for this seismic revelation. I would have somehow been asked to do a Ted Talk about my hilarious yet deeply profound experience of giving up alcohol, which would have gone viral, touching the hearts and minds of not only the masses but also almost every world leader. For some reason, it would be me who said something that no other human being—speaker or best-selling author—had ever said about alcohol before, and the blue touch paper would have been lit. No need to ban alcohol because the world would immediately have no desire to drink the moment they heard my words. The narcissistic fantasy of a fledgling soberite, thinking they had now transcended to a higher plane.

Then someone came on who actually did have something interesting and witty to say: the presenter, Adrian Chiles. He'd been invited to speak on the back of his excellent documentary 'Drinkers Like Me', in which he is refreshingly candid about his own drinking, straightforwardly and humorously exploring the effects of alcohol on our health (and his own) as well as on society. What I related to both in the documentary and in what he said that day at the festival was that heavy drinking, dependency, whatever you want to call it, has in many ways now become 'normal'.

Beyond the challenges of treating alcoholism, he explains, the wider problem is that dangerous levels of drinking and dependency are commonplace. So, we need to talk about that and without fear of being stigmatised if we hold our hands up and admit to being one of those people who drinks too much. His declaring that he might be one of those people is hugely courageous. Adrian's most powerfully vulnerable moment came when he described how he was trying to moderate, using an app to keep tabs on how many units he consumes a week. He said he was regularly passing the maximum recommended levels and that keeping some kind of control had become an occupying endeavour.

I noticed several people in the audience smiling empathetically, because, like me, they know that trying to moderate when you've travelled so far off the main drag and into the wilderness with that particular companion is tough. Not impossible, but I know it would be exhausting for me to try. I know that the effort would consume me and that I'd almost certainly fail. At some point, maybe not immediately but weeks or months down the line, I would be back with my bosom buddy and off on another adventure into the wilderness we would go.

The question which immediately comes to mind when I'm tempted to contemplate the moderation thing, having been such a heavy drinker, is why would I do that? To attempt to do so, for me, would be to say life is less without alcohol, so I must find a way to have some. That experiencing the effects of alcohol holds some importance to me, because it helps me to feel this or that, or to do this or that in a more pleasant or enhanced way. Life for me now is so vastly improved by experiencing it alcohol-free, that to risk it for alcohol would be to risk having something precious taken away.

My freedom.

I left that Sunday afternoon and headed back home, feeling quite different, like I'd just completed my first day in a new job. I had met all these new people, people who knew so much more than me, and I realised how much more there must still be for me to learn. And, indeed, there was.

Adventures in Sober Land

Chapter 8

Maintaining the work/booze balance

It started to slowly dawn on me, during the last ten years of my dependency on alcohol, that the focus of my energy had not been on maintaining a healthy work/life balance but rather on sustaining an unhealthy work/booze balance. I managed to fool myself for quite some time that because I didn't drink in the morning, nor on workdays or at lunchtime, and because I had no real craving to drink when my mind was 'on the job', somehow any dependence I had was normal. In other words, I was normally dependent. Interesting concept. As you will see, my dependency was anything but normal. By way of demonstration, I want to take you through my work/booze schedule in the form of a 24-hour clock.

***

10.30pm—Bottle of red wine nearly finished save for one half-glass held in reserve to have with the mandatory slice of cheese or piece of chocolate, or both, having made sure the children are asleep, the front door is locked and most lights switched off.

11.00pm—Finish the half glass of red wine with cheese or chocolate while flicking through social media or agonising over my Fantasy Football team.

11.15pm—Take cup of tea to bed, but aware it makes the prospect of cleaning my teeth less likely as I will be in bed drinking cup of tea and might nod off.

11.30pm—Drinking tea in bed, trying to stay awake while I watch something on my iPad, but relieved that I'm so tired because to turn the light off still awake might trigger a dread of being left alone with my thoughts.

11.45pm—I'm starting to drift off, come to, then drift off again until I know the time has finally come to drag my iPad across the duvet and onto the floor and haul my arm to the bedside lamp to switch off the light. I'm so tired now that I know I'll attain my goal of falling into a completely unconscious state in just a few moments.

2.30am—I wake suddenly to a delightful mix of dehydration and self-loathing. Heart racing, mouth as a parched as an orangutan's that's mislaid its wine, I lie there in the dark in complete despair at who I've become, at the cycle of alcohol dependence I'm in, and of the terrible mistakes I've made in my life—you get the picture. I desperately search for the 'thought ritual' I use at this, the witching hour, to escape my present hell for another twenty-four hours. This is the story which will eventually send me off to sleep again.

I am on the edge of some sort of rainforest somewhere in southeast Asia, up on a mountainside overlooking a golden beach below and an endless sea, empty save for a few small islands glimmering in the sunlight some way off. Here on the mountainside, surrounded by lush trees and cascading waterfalls, I'm in a luxury cabin made of bamboo, which has its own private view of a small lake into which overwhelmingly peaceful sounds of water falling into water drift over me. Other luxury cabins are nearby. I'm in a kind of sanctuary, a beautiful rehabilitation centre where I've been taken and laid upon soft pillows in the middle of the hut. I'd been found and carried here one terrible night when I'd finally collapsed and the truth of my despair had caught up with me. I am left to sleep for days to rebuild my strength, and eventually I'll wake in this oasis of peace where other people, who've reached this same place of despair, are slowly rebuilding their lives too. It is in this place that I know I will learn to never drink again, where all my anxiety and depression will be drawn from me in some sort of exhumation, and from which I'll one day walk away as a man transformed, healthy and at peace. I never reach the end of the story; I'm always still lying on those pillows in the middle of the cabin as I fade once more into unconsciousness. It is this story that saves me every night.

6.30am—The alarm goes off. The effects of yet another mild-to-moderate hangover linger over me, enveloping me in a veil of deep tiredness that comes from years of never truly feeling rested. I also feel just plain ill, but never enough not to get up and drag my body into a new day. To make myself a cup of tea, to shower, to get ready, to grab a coffee for the road and head out towards another day of delivering training with an energy I can't imagine generating at this unearthly hour. I say to myself that today will be the day I will stop drinking, perhaps forever.

8.30am—Arrive at destination. Bacon sandwich and coffee consumed in the car. Vaguely feeling like I am a functioning creature of some sort. I can't say a human being at this stage: a simpler life form, perhaps, such as the Mycoplasma, the very simplest of bacteria that doesn't even have a cell wall. I just wish I could fully clear the clouds still shrouding my brain. I need another coffee.

9.30am—And we're off. I'm running a training course, seemingly at peace with myself, focused, energised and in control. I am not sure what happens in that hour before, but each time I seem to find a way of climbing out of myself, brushing myself down and stepping once more into the spotlight. I wonder if it has something to do with having spent part of my life in the performing arts, or with my training as an actor, but there's something about the effects of 'doctor theatre' which sees me through every performance, no matter how terrible I feel. The show must go on, and all that. Except that I know, within my heart, that I'm accumulating so much internal damage that if I carry on like this it will catch up with me one day, probably very suddenly when I'm in full swing. I also know, each time I catch my reflection in the mirror, that the results of my habit are, bit by bit, starting to take shape; or, to be precise, starting to take over my shape. Overweight, puffy eyes, pallid, at least until lunchtime when I start to rouge up a bit.

11.00am—Coffee break. I'm chatting with the participants on the course and I'm probably now at my optimum. As we chat, I quietly promise myself that I will not drink again until the weekend, and even then it will be moderately.

1.00pm—Lunchtime. I am sitting with the group and having lunch. Having a salad, in fact; no carbs because I've resolved that not only will I not be drinking for the rest of the week, but that I will lose weight by eating healthily and going to the gym, which I'm already a member of but attend perhaps twice a month on average. Great. I have a plan. No alcohol during the week and drinking moderately at the weekend, except for maybe when it's a big night out, for example.

3.00 pm—Coffee break. I might have a drink tomorrow, Tuesday, but not tonight. Maybe I'll do one day on, one day off during the week, and then drink fairly moderately at the weekend (or at least drink 'normally heavily' on Saturday night) but stop drinking all together from about fourish on Sunday. That way I will be good for Monday and the start of the week, when I will do, as I say, the one day on, one day off thing. Or maybe the whole week off, whole weekend on thing, or whatever it was I thought was a great idea earlier.

5.00pm—End of course. Largely great feedback and a good day had by all. The show is over, the curtains have come down. I make my way back to the dressing room in my mind and quietly sit for a moment. Okay, tomorrow will be my off day and tonight my day on day, instead of the other way around as planned earlier, because tomorrow I am working from home and I just really feel I deserve a drink tonight. However, I will have just a couple, one when I get home, and one with the meal. Half a bottle, max. And tomorrow will *definitely* be my day off on that 'one day off, one day on' timetable. Then on Sunday, I will plan to do the whole week off, and then do the drink 'moderately heavily' thing at the weekend. That's what I'd agreed with myself. Isn't it?

6.30pm—Had a beer when I got in, so this glass of wine I'm pouring now is actually my first 'drink' drink of the two I said I'd have. It's just that I like to have a glass of wine while I'm making the food. It's what *makes* making the food. That's why, on my days off from drinking, I'll eat much earlier and choose something that can be made without any real thought. How about salads with tuna or cold chicken on my days off?

7.00pm—I pour one more glass of wine than planned pre-food because I had to go up and help my wife with something upstairs, or one of my children, and that has put dinner on hold for half an hour. Plus I also need to get an email off to a client. But that's okay, three glasses of wine and a small beer is manageable really, and a hell of a lot better than the usual bottle I drink per night during the week. And definitely better than the 'almost two bottles' on a Saturday night, for God's sake.

8.00pm—Just finished the meal and we're getting into this box set. Feeling that nice fuzzy feeling which I know I'll pay the price for later. But, rather like that 'thought ritual' I go through in the early hours of the morning, I can use this moment of squiffiness to escape the future and quite simply say **** it. There's less than half a bottle of wine left now. As I'm not drinking tomorrow night, finishing this means I get a clean break and ensures I won't have anything hanging around open to tempt me when I get back from work. So, just as my wife does with her white, I do with my red and I pour another large glass.

9.00pm—Check on the children and in a soppy/stern manner tell them it's time for bed. Their resistance triggers an overreaction in me which leads to irascible tellings-off, basically for just being children. I then apologise for my reaction, give them lots of kisses goodnight, and make my way back down to the cause of my impatience: the quarter-to third-full bottle of red wine.

10.00pm—I have topped my glass up once since the large refill earlier because I don't want to run out too early and I know I can't open another bottle—or can I? I mean sometimes I do open a second, but usually I manage to hold off by having a cheeky beer in between if absolutely necessary. Tonight, I will not have that filler beer. That's a good sign, isn't it?

10.30pm—Bottle of red wine nearly finished save for one-half glass held in reserve to have with the mandatory slice of cheese or piece of chocolate, or both, after having made sure the children are asleep, the front door is locked and most lights switched off.

***

The sober 24-hour clock.

What can I say about this very different clock? Well, the highs and lows of being human still punctuate the hours, but here are some key differences.

10.45pm—Cup of tea in bed followed by cleaning of teeth. Watching something on the iPad or reading, then turning off bedside light and loving the feeling of being deeply tired.

6.30am—Alarm goes off. Never cease to be amazed by how well I have slept (generally) and how much energy I seem to have for the day ahead.

5.00pm. End of course. Largely great feedback and a good day had by all. The show is over, the curtains have come down. I make my way back to the dressing room in my mind and quietly sit for a moment. I'm looking forward to getting home to see the children, to making a meal with perhaps an alcohol-free beer or two to keep me company, to eating at around seven, doing some writing, watching something, or obsessing about my fantasy football team (because I am an obsessive person and that has nothing to do with alcohol). All that sort of thing. Always amazed at how much I can get done in the evening. Tomorrow I'm working from home so I can catch up with boring admin, but I can also get down to the gym, which I go to about eight times a month now. Or go for a run, which I do at least once a week.

***

The joy of working away in Alcohol World

I am approaching a large country hotel up a long tree-lined drive, or perhaps I'm winding my way through the streets of a city here in the UK, or somewhere in Europe or indeed much further afield. Maybe I'm on a train that is just pulling in, or on a plane that's just landed. Whatever and wherever it might be, this week I'm running a two or three-day course with participants unleashed from their everyday working lives, either looking forward to or not looking forward to the training ahead, but almost all up for some time out, to let their hair down a bit. This is great because right now I'm a fully paid-up member of Alcohol World.

Before I left home I had a little glass of something to send me on my way, to give me the zip I needed until top up time on arrival at my destination—unless it's a long journey by train or plane, in which case all bets are off and there'll two or more consumed before I hit the bar later. As I enter the hotel reception, its warm and inviting ambience appears to me like a drinks menu, insisting I order something very soon. I'm feeling ridiculously excited at the prospect of having this time out from my everyday routine because there is absolutely no way that I won't be having a drink every evening I'm here. Indeed, it's stated in the 2nd Amendment of Alcohol World's constitution: the right to bear alcohol when staying in hotels or going on holiday. The notion of not drinking in the evening is therefore utterly incomprehensible. The only downer is that because I'm working each day, I will have to think about how much I consume. I will, to some extent, take my lead from how fun (or not) the person is with whom I'm running the course, or indeed how lush the participants are, but either way I will drink. And while I'm away, all possible guilt about drinking or attempts 'not to drink tonight' will be joyously abandoned.

I reach my room, do my two-minute unpack and change, and then I'm off on my way along the corridor to the lift and down to paradise, course notes in hand. I notice a pair of suit trousers wedged and scrunched around the door handle of someone's bedroom door, down the corridor from me, and have a little chuckle to myself. How on earth did someone's trousers manage to end up there, one leg hanging forlornly and one tangled around a handle? I have this vision of someone running around the hotel in boxer shorts at this very moment, completely drunk, desperately searching for them.

The bar is rather swish, exuding the same inviting ambience as the reception area, except this place doesn't just feel like a drinks menu—it is one. Shelves of inviting bottles sparkle under the soft lighting behind the bar. Staff move with speed and dexterity between uncorked bottles, glasses, beer taps, and guests. Guests transmit various states of bottled impatience while awaiting their turn to be served, apparently unconcerned except for the gently tapping foot or finger. That'll be me in a moment, so I carefully look for any possible gaps at the bar before I land and lock on. When I look back at this scene, of me approaching that bar and a thousand other bars like it, I see it as my being drawn to a large charging point in the middle of the room where I must plug myself in. Get my fix. The times I've done the same—lurk twitchily at the bar, waiting for that fix—when out with colleagues and friends, too.

It really is a "fix." I might as well say, as the bartender finally looks up, "Hi, can I have two lines of coke please, one spliff and an ecstasy tab? Thanks. Oh, and two packets of crisps for the one having the spliff."

Can you, the reader, see any difference except for the randomness by which one drug happens to be legal and the others not? If I pull back further, now looking down on this scene from afar, taking in the entire room, I see myself at the bar, this quietly dependent man, tapping his fingers whilst looking around as if he has all the time in the world. I see myself watching as people move like waves, first lapping against the bar and then receding to settle in pools at nearby tables, replenishing their various states of mind. I am in awe at the sleight of hand that has entirely normalised this ritual.

So here I am at a table, sipping a pint of lager, because at half seven a beer somehow feels less hardcore than a glass of red. On a workday evening out with colleagues that first glass of red wine might be something taken when just going through for dinner or, better still, ordered in the restaurant when perusing the menu. I look around the room and wonder how many of the people here will be on tomorrow's course. And, more to the point, how many of them will be drinkers? The more the merrier as far as I'm concerned, since they'll offer the best kind of camouflage there is for a drinker like me.

My great friend and colleague Anthony (he of the London Palladium all those years earlier), arrives and our relationship is such that we start laughing even before we've even said anything. He likes a drink too, so this is going to be a fun two days. He puts his glass of white wine on the table. For some reason, with him, it looks a perfectly acceptable drink to be having, and not too early. We've known each other for over thirty years and though he, like many of my friends and colleagues, appears to drink as much as I do, somehow this doesn't seem to offer him any problems. Whereas drinking has gradually eroded my life, his has flourished. I don't mean our physical health—heavy drinking doesn't discriminate in that regard—no, I'm talking about the choices we make. Mine with money, relationships, and quite simply how I have spent my time, which has led me down one path, and his choices with money, relationships, and how he's spent his time, down another.

As we know, drinking was my way of dealing with seriously uncomfortable feelings, whereas I can only imagine that with Anthony it has simply enhanced already comfortable ones. That saying "Never drink to be happy, only to be happier" comes to mind. So, am I to conclude that he and all my heavy-ish drinking friends and colleagues must be 'normally' dependent, yet I, and others like me, are abnormally so? Maybe that is the truth. If so, I'd love to know where the line between the two lies, and how we can determine when that line might have been crossed.

As we unwind, Anthony and I go through the back catalogue of the most excruciating/hysterical moments we have experienced when delivering training courses:

1. Anthony squatting down, back to the audience, to sort out some cables at the front of the room and ripping his trousers along the entire length of his backside.
2. My demoing how to have a challenging conversation with a colleague, with my flies wide open, in front of a group of about ten participants sitting extremely close together and *directly* in front of me. Underpants a vivid red and my demo extremely earnest.
3. My running a workshop on personal impact in front of about 250 female image consultants, where I have the bright idea of asking them to stick their tongues out and write their names in the air with them because you need to warm up all your vocal tools. I cannot tell you what on earth prompted me to ask them to do this, en masse and facing me, but I will never forget the experience.

4. Anthony being roared on by participants in the bar at the end of the first day of a two-day training course, doing a headstand while downing a pint of beer in one. Seriously impressive and seriously much younger at the time, when credibility was of secondary importance.

5. My running a bullying and harassment course with actor colleagues helping to bring contentious workplace scenarios to life. When I asked the audience what might be wrong about men still having pictures of topless women up in their office (it was a very blokey construction company), one woman stood up and said this was political correctness gone mad and she'd happily show off her tits at work.

6. My talking about the need to be yourself when presenting (and not coming across as overly coached, as I felt Tony Blair appeared to be later in his premiership), not remotely realising that the client contact, watching from the back, used to be his speechwriter.

7. My role-playing with a participant to help them practice delivering difficult feedback to me as if I was their work colleague, only to encounter an internal facilitator asking me not only how it felt receiving this message but, extraordinarily, how it tasted. All I could think of to say was 'salty'.

8. Doing an improvised demo with an actor colleague in front of participants on how to shift your personal status in any given situation. We chose a doctor/patient scenario, and, in the heat of the moment, it all got out of hand. I asked him to bend over so I could inspect his anal wart.

9. Co-running a course during which I put participants into groups to discuss an element of theory amongst themselves. While I was doing this, my colleague sidled up to me and told me she had farted. I wasn't sure what my colleague wanted me to say or do when presented with this information. Was it a hint that I should move before being struck down, look for air freshener or simply enquire as to whether there was anything I could do to support her? Undeterred by my momentary need for reflection she said again, "I have farted", but this time much more loudly, ripping through all discussion in the room.

10. My dashing into the loo, during a break in a training course I was running, and while sitting in a state of deep relief in the cubicle, hearing three or four pairs of stilettos entering the loo accompanied by female voices. I sat there completely frozen throughout. When all had left and quiet had descended, I moved like that mad monkey from Hangover Part 2 again, and escaped just as two more women entered. I never looked back.

When I look at the above list, I would say that the flies wide open, the alphabet tongues, the anal wart drama and the dash into the women's loos might not have happened had I not been impeded by the marginal losses which a hangover imposes on our ability to respond optimally in such situations. Indeed, I might have: dealt with my colleagues need to tell me she had farted more promptly; thought that Tony Blair might be liked by some people; come up with a more appropriate response to how someone's difficult message tasted, and been able to offer a witty riposte to the woman in the audience who said she would happily get her tits out at work. I will never know. I am still waiting, as a resident of Sober Land, for such challenges to arise to test my mettle.

Anyway, back to our hotel bar, where the client is coming to the table with a G&T in hand while Anthony and I are still weeping with laughter over our escapades. Thank God she's drinking as well. I quickly order a glass of red and we discuss tomorrow's schedule, along with any troublesome participants we should look out for, and generally look to assure our client that the day will be a great day. I am good (at least I think I am) at seeming to be completely 'on it'. Professional, vaguely witty, incisive. In truth, I'm probably ever so slightly slurring and ever so slightly manic. Finally we head through to the restaurant, which is a relief because I really could do with another drink. The one I ordered on her arrival was emptied long before our discussion ended and I didn't want to look too desperate, thus I held off ordering another.

Unfortunately, once 'trapped' at the dinner table, our client suggests we order by the glass as she only wants one more, max. How dull and mean is that? I was hoping we might share a bottle, with Anthony and I demolishing most of it. Instead I have to make that one glass see me all the way through three courses, leaving me with one miserly sip for the chocolate cheesecake. I find this deeply depressing. Fast forward to around half ten, Anthony and I are back in the bar, mustering up the courage to resist ordering another drink and heading instead to our respective rooms. I am feeling a little squiffy, but—if I'm honest—not quite at the optimum level of squiffiness I would like. These are fine margins, particularly on a work night. With our client having retired to bed immediately after dinner, I'd knocked back another couple of reds in double time and now find myself in the lift with Anthony, swaying ever so slightly and saying something fairly outrageous to him that only very good friends can say and get away with.

Our rooms happen to be on the same floor. As we make our way along the corridor, we spot those bloody trousers, still hanging from the door handle of that bedroom door. While giggling and snorting, which must be delightful for those trying to sleep, we attempt to discuss whether we should knock on the door in case they do indeed belong to the occupant of that room. Some poor guy's sitting there in that room, certain he's lost them, and fretting over having to attend his meeting tomorrow in a pair of shorts. But what happens if they're not his?

I bid Anthony goodnight and enter my room. I really could do with a nightcap just to send me into the deep sleep I crave, sure that I will not wake in a pool of despair later. Isn't it strange how being in a hotel offers me release from the guilt I live with every day back in the 'real world'? I decide that I'll order a large red from room service, and so what if there's a £5 charge applied. It's better than the embarrassment of returning to the bar and happening to bump into Anthony, who might have forgotten something or, indeed, the client. I just don't know what I would say. Perhaps that's the difference between Anthony and me and all my other drinking friends. He and they wouldn't feel the need for just one more. They probably wouldn't feel the need for one before leaving home, either. But then again I lived with this secret for a long time without anyone suspecting a thing. Unless someone reaches out, we'll never know what someone is going through when they quietly close the door behind them.

I get into my pyjamas, the same ones which will one day become magical, and proceed to get my notes and documents together for tomorrow. I set my alarm while I wait for the delivery of my tranquilliser. Damn! I suddenly remember that I'd forgotten to iron my shirt, so I shuffle over to the wardrobe. As I take it out, crumpled from the hanger, I accidentally knock my suit jacket onto the floor. But not my suit trousers. No, not my suit trousers because my suit trousers are not there. Where the hell are my suit trousers? For God's sake, I have a crumpled shirt and I have a suit jacket, but no bloody trousers. I rush to my case because I might have put them in there by mistake and not on the hanger with my jacket when I left home. But they're not there either, nor are they in the bathroom. Or anywhere. I only have in my possession the very narrowest of drainpipe jeans, which I'm wearing, or my pyjama bottoms. Neither will cut it for running a corporate training course for a blue-chip company. They're very suit-orientated at this particular company. Perhaps Anthony might have a spare pair? I go to call him and then suddenly it hits me.

I *have* seen my trousers this evening.

Dear God, I thought they looked familiar during the snorting and weeping along the corridor just fifteen minutes ago. Yet the absurdity of a pair of trousers hanging off a door handle in the middle of a hotel blinded me from the, well, blindingly obvious. The trousers which have hung out there for hours now, exposing their owner to utter humiliation, are MY trousers! How did they end up there? I don't understand, and the not understanding bit isn't helped by the fact that I suddenly realise I'm more squiffy than I thought, and that the large red that's on its way may not be such a good idea. Either way, I must go and get them, now, immediately.

I creep to my door. This is unnecessary, on reflection, because of course no one can see or hear me at this point. I leave my room and tiptoe slowly along the corridor towards my trousers, obediently still hanging there. I move as if approaching a sleeping creature of some sort that I dare not wake. I finally reach them and gently unhook them from the door handle. It gradually becomes clearer to me what happened. When I made my way to my room on arrival, my case in one hand and my suit slung over my shoulder (feeling quite cool, I seem to remember), I did at one point brush closely against what I thought was the wall when turning suddenly, with the manic movement of the gently inebriated, because I thought I might have gone past my room. In that instant, the belt hoop of my trousers must have hooked silently onto the door handle and pulled my trousers off their hanger.

Anyway, I now have my trousers, thank the Lord, and I turn and run back to the door of my room. Which is shut. Locked. And I don't have my key. I feel a strangely calm feeling of complete panic. As if this is all happening to someone else and I am watching on. What am I going to do? I hear the ding of the lift suddenly ring out. Someone's going to step out and see me standing in my nightwear, holding a pair of trousers in my hand. It could be a course participant. It could be the client! I spot a broom cupboard and wonder if that might be an option, but at that moment a figure from the lift does indeed emerge. But wait, it's a member of staff.

It's room service. My need for another glass of red wine might well have saved me. Drinking IS a good thing. He will let me into my room. And I will celebrate finding my trousers by drinking that large glass of wine, with no one the wiser about what had happened either in the loss or in the finding of the trousers. Yes, I will celebrate and then I will pass out. But before that, I am going to have to suffer the humiliation of trying to explain why I am here, as I am, in this ridiculous state. I smile and brace myself for yet another excruciating episode of life here in Alcohol World.

***

When I look back on that night and all those other countless nights—which were variants of it but without the trousers, if you get my drift—I can't believe that I pulled it off. That I managed to heave my 'just a bit too hungover for a workday' head off the pillow, my bloated body into the shower, and my puffy face to the mirror to be shaved. That I folded up and stuffed my self-loathing into my suitcase and managed to haul myself downstairs for breakfast. That I heaved my anxiety into the training room, where I wrote up the day's agenda for as long as I could before anyone else arrived. Really, how did I do it? I look back on me then, from here in Sober Land, and I feel deeply sad for the person I had become and for the fear I so often felt around my belief that this would be me forever. I'm also proud of how I managed to keep going. That, amidst the hell I was in for so long, there was still some ethical self in the former me, trying his best to give everything he could to what he was being paid to do.

If this is you right now, still giving of your best while caught in the slipstream of dependency, I can tell you that you have it within you to change. It is that part of you that can be your North Star to guide you out of the darkness. Use it.

I still remember walking down the corridor that morning, trudging towards the lift, utterly disappointed in myself and full of promises that I already knew I would break. I remember being at breakfast with Anthony and telling him that those trousers we snorted about last night were in fact my trousers, and then us snorting even more loudly all the way from the full English breakfast into the training room. Doctor theatre once more took centre stage. I remember we did a great job that day and had fun too with the participants, and I remember a few of them coming into the room that morning, at the beginning of day one, with the sheepish demeanour of having had far too many the night before. I remember thinking that they would be good undergrowth to hide in later if indeed I did break my promise, which I knew I would.

Now, as I sit here in my hotel room at 9.30pm, with a cup of tea on the table next to me, magic pyjamas still in my case, suit trousers hanging, boringly I admit, in the wardrobe next to my 'ironed' shirt, I think of all those people downstairs right now at the bar knocking back their various drinks, plugged into an evening of relaxation and mild abandonment. These are the moments when I feel as if I might be missing out on something, on the warm glow of bar lights and flowing wine and the hum of voices engaged in debate or laughter. The telling of stories, of gossip and intrigue, of business deals being made or the first sparks of attraction rising from the enticing flames of alcohol. In the past, I would have been right there in the thick of it all, but after dinner tonight with two of my colleagues and our participants, I said goodnight and made my way up to my room. Where's the adventure in that, I hear you say? Where's the reward in missing out?

Well, the adventure is in the 'not' drinking, and in the experiencing of everything as it actually is. It's in the experience of taking in the world through a prism of feelings that are real. Feelings often so ablaze with energy, giving me overwhelming enthusiasm and hope, but sometimes depleted, leaving a certain emptiness and despondency. Then again, at times, experiencing just the need for a quiet reflection and a deep desire to be alone, like tonight, for example. And that's the reward. Feeling good about the choices I make. That's why, ultimately, I know I am not missing out.

And, of course, the adventure is in doing what I am doing right now. Writing. I would not have come close to doing this when I lived in Alcohol World. I would have thought

about it, but never have got around to doing it. What's
more, I have already written probably two-thirds of this book
on planes and trains (automobiles would be pushing it) and
in hotel bars. Yes, I love sitting in bars with my ginger beers
or alcohol-free lagers with the buzz of chatter around me, or
in cafés, waiting for connections. In hotel rooms too, in
silence, last thing at night or first thing in the morning
because I've already fully recharged long before the alarm
goes off. The adventure is in being at my best when I
deliver the work I'm being paid to deliver, looking vaguely
healthy, and therefore qualified to coach people on
personal impact because I no longer resemble a baby
hippo. I still laugh a lot and I'm still sociable when I relax
with colleagues and clients at the end of the day. I am not
saying it is always easy. It isn't, and I have to be on my
guard when I start to flag and haven't eaten, or if I feel
thirsty and tired and I'm sitting in an airport lounge, for
example. The edgy feelings rise, but so far I've always
found a way through by accepting these feelings and
ploughing on through, much as one does when it suddenly
rains and you have no coat but you just keep walking. And
then eventually the sun comes out again.

I don't have a regular hours job, nor do I work in an office,
but if I did I absolutely would've been one of those who
rushed from their place of work at five and headed straight

for the nearest bar to have one or three or more for the road. I'd have been one of those who'd have picked something up to eat on the way home a few too many times, who would have missed many of the family rituals I should have been part of, and all their accompanying responsibilities. I'd have been among those who slumped into bed, fell into restless sleep, and then suddenly found the alarm going off far too soon for comfort. When it comes to the life of the dependent drinker, all the symptoms are the same, wherever you work and whatever you do.

Here's an article I wrote on the subject a few months into my sobriety.

The Work/Booze balance

"Who's going for a drink later?" It's an innocuous question asked millions of times every working day. And sure enough, a few hours later, as the day draws to an end, doors are flung open and people flow towards their favourite haunts to unwind and unpick the happenings of the day.

Others skip the invitation and head straight home after picking up a cheeky bottle of something to snuggle up to later. Amongst the cooking of their evening meal, putting children to bed, dealing with never-ending domestic 'stuff', the warm glow of drink lights up the evening. Sometimes—indeed often—work 'stuff' continues to interrupt via buzzing, pinging phones, from which emails or message exchanges carry on a little too late into the evening for comfort.

These are the habits of millions of hard-working people simply doing what normal people do. Coming into work in not quite the state they had hoped, just a little more often than intended. The grey area drinkers, like me, neither off the scale nor really on top of that moderation malarkey.

So, does having even just a mild hangover really make any difference to our working day?

A little cloudy with the prospect of showers later. It's 9am and frankly, some people are a bit too bouncy for their own good! Having navigated the maddening crowds to reach the office, the crammed trains or motorways, or the school drop off—the last thing you need is fully charged bunnies coming at you with ridiculously bright 'Good mornings'. The act of remotely trying to match their energy is not only exhausting but bloody irritating. You finally reach your desk. You now just need fifteen minutes to get yourself together, quietly. Have a coffee, finish off your cold bacon roll, browse your emails. But work doesn't play ball. You have that meeting with a new client in five minutes, a member of your team really needs to talk to you, your boss really needs to talk to you *now*—you really need to talk to you! Or there's the briefing you promised to give or hear first thing. Whatever it is, you need to 'switch on'. And that's the problem. The clouds don't clear that quickly. It's as if you physically need to manufacture high winds to move them.

Generally, we get away with it—or do we? Is getting away with it the point, anyway? It's the price we pay over the long term, the things we miss, the choices we make which affect the people around us. In high-performance sport, they talk about marginal gains. Well, even with a mild hangover, for me it's about marginal losses.

There are a few marginal losses I can think of straight away, which start to accumulate when we are in this state of active recovery. To start with, just not being fully present. I mean, how can we be? Too much energy and focus are being channelled inwards to really notice what is happening beyond us, particularly where the more nuanced stuff is concerned. When we're fully present, we make more accurate observations, listen at a deeper level, ask more pertinent questions, and make people feel more valued. Energy and enthusiasm are also seriously depleted in recovery mode, and therefore our ability to bring people with us and get things done is so much more of a struggle. Yes, our 'compensating' energy does a pretty good job, but it's never as good as the real thing.

And how about our ability to manage our emotional state when hungover? We'll almost certainly be more reactive. We may not even notice it, but somewhere along the line, even at a non-verbal level, we will transmit a little more intolerance, for example. A little less 'control'. That smile you push through won't always balance the books in the minds of others.

These marginal losses are of course all due to the energy we have to put in just to get back to normal, versus the amount of energy we'd otherwise have to excel.

I can think of many more marginal losses, as I am sure you can too, but I won't go on about them here. Perhaps, instead, those of us who can relate to what might be called 'mild hangover syndrome' (or MHS—sorry can't resist an acronym) might take a moment to reflect on their own work-booze balance. Looking back, there's absolutely no doubt in my mind that the marginal losses I created had an impact in some way or another, either on myself or those around me. I will probably never really know entirely in what way, or by how much.

But multiply 'me' (God forbid) a million times over, all creating our own little losses, and I guess this might be a discussion worth having?

Chapter 9

Lisbon

Why Lisbon, you might ask? Is there some secret sanctuary where dependent drinkers converge every year to break the shackles of addiction? No, it's where I got off my face on cannabis just before boarding a plane once, and where also, years later, the first classic encounter between booze and my belly took place bang in the middle of the ANA business lounge.

It's also where I spent my last holiday with my father when I was thirty-three years old.

I still feel a strong emotional connection to the city. I know my father loved it and, in particular, the countryside and the mountains of Sintra about an hour or so away. Lisbon is, like my father was, intrinsically romantic. Wistfully romantic, a little lost and out on its own. But very beautiful in a wonderfully imperfect way.

It's also where a maelstrom of emotions converged within me on that first trip. Those darned feelings again: my

Achilles heel and the force that drove my drinking. And, at the time, the smoking of copious amounts of weed.

Before you wonder where this is heading, I want to ask if you have your own 'Lisbon'? Your place or time when looking back, you can see that you really did need help, and if you'd had it, perhaps you wouldn't have turned down the path you did? From here in Sober Land, I can see that, for me, it was that place and it was that week. Australia, too, come to think of it, less than ten years earlier. Two defining places which indelibly marked the landscape of my mind.

I had flown out with my girlfriend (later to be wife) the week between Christmas and New Year. My sister Jenny had died a few months earlier in October of a brain tumour at the age of forty-three. She had lived her life fast and 'high', but she was so wonderfully ballsy, courageous and kind. And completely clean living, ironically, when she died. I wish I'd been able to spend more time with her and to tell her that she wasn't the only one. We were more alike than she ever knew. I believe we really could have helped each other. The year before that, exactly to the month, my friend and mentor Glyn had died from an alcohol-precipitated fall. A friend addicted to alcohol who I'd been drawn into helping almost inevitably, now I look back on it. After all, I was already well-versed, from a young age, in playing the part of the co-dependent. I put him into rehab so many times and endured so many crazy games of 'lies and seek', but he was also responsible for helping me to at least begin to believe I could write. He was a such a kind and generous person who just so happened to be deeply dependent on alcohol. I will never forget him.

So I did write, albeit sporadically, up until he, my sister and father all died in quick succession over two years. Or, to be precise, three Octobers. It has struck me that it's only now, since giving up alcohol, that I've started writing again. Over twenty years later. Any guesses as to why this might be?

I sometimes wonder what might have happened had someone stopped me just before I scored a big junk of cannabis off some stranger in a dimly lit back street that first night in Lisbon, when I'd visited with my then-girlfriend. Not that anything terrible happened as a consequence (bar my boarding our plane home while off my tree—more about that later), but that holiday very simply symbolises how grubby things had got. I still speculate about how things might have unfolded for me if someone I knew, at that moment in that back street, had grabbed me by the collar, pulled me into some café, sat me down and told me what I needed to hear:

"You do know why you're doing this, don't you? It's not just these deaths that have escalated your consumption of weed and booze over the last year or so. It's something more fundamental than that. Your mental health is shot. I know you know this, deep down. You've been heading towards this moment for a very long time, doing anything you could do to distract yourself from facing up to the difficult feelings you've endured, to escape the troubled mind you've lived with since you were fourteen—the one which has resulted in relationships ending, over the ensuing years, with wonderful women who truly loved you. You drink to mask the depression and anxiety which has caused you to sabotage every professional opportunity you ever created—fantastic openings you felled one after the other with your complete lack of self-belief and self-esteem. This gradual build-up of substance abuse, this manic obsession with creating new concepts, games, ideas, business ventures, you name it—it's all an attempt to run away from feelings and towards the need to feel self-worth. Well, it's now time to stop. It's now time to get help. It's now time to talk and to take the first step to change your life. It's time to set yourself free."

That would've been a useful intervention from anybody, but when I look back at that moment in that darkened alleyway, there's one person above all others I wish had dragged me

146

out into the light and confronted me. My father. He was there in Lisbon that very evening, out somewhere out with a friend, but the truth is, he was incapable. He was, himself, utterly lost, orbiting the world somewhere far away, constantly escaping into writing music he could never finish. I am convinced he, like my mother to this day, had issues he just could not express. For all his gentleness and sensitivity, he just didn't have it in him to reach out to his son and lead him down that other path. So, when his death did come, ten months after Lisbon, it felt like something out of a dream. I was already gone. As he slipped away, I watched on from the corner of the hospital room like a wraith even though I was in fact at his bedside, holding his hand as he took his last rattling breath. Emphysema took him after a lifetime of heavy smoking. An addiction he too couldn't free himself from.

So, take it from me. If you can relate to the exhausting and overwhelming nature of mental illness, whether mild, middling or extreme, then know this—alcohol really, really, really doesn't help. It just makes it all so much worse.

From that night, when no one had intervened, I went on to spend the next twenty years digging myself deeper and deeper into ever-thickening layers of alcohol dependence. A crazy excavation that went on long after the dust of those

crumbled lines of dope and coke had blown away, for which
I am still paying the price to this day. But I address the
difficult times from a position of clarity now, a place of hope
and a sense of freedom that cannot be explained in words.
If you choose to do the same, you will know what I mean,
just as all those who I have met along the way know too.

***

The rest of the holiday was great—heady, intoxicating and
spent with my father in restaurants and bars, climbing in the
hills of Sintra, or walking the streets of Lisbon and visiting
its historical sights. I remember dancing with my girlfriend
on New Year's Eve in this unassuming restaurant as my
father watched on, unwell, but with what seemed a truly
peaceful gaze. The owners had staged an impromptu
'dance-off' as we approached midnight. We fought other
couples in a 'battle of the dancers', where we comically out
spun and out-leapt everyone, narrowly missing tables and
human legs. And the winnings? A large bottle of something
non-alcoholic. After all that! At the time I remember both of
us were terribly put out by what we saw as a complete
insult to our outstanding exertions. However, not all was
lost. After all, I still had that large-but-shrinking lump of
cannabis in my pocket and a good many bars to visit before
the holiday was up.

But then it *was* up. Suddenly, it seemed. The rest of the week had flown by in a blur—utterly unsurprisingly, of course. We arrived at the airport early evening, having bid farewell to my father in town and made our way anxiously to the check-in desk. We were bad flyers and had already downed a few drinks to calm the nerves, but more were required. We wanted to get to the departure lounge ASAP. As we stood impatiently in the queue, I must have put my hand in my pocket to check what change I had, or something. And there it was—the unmistakable presence of what was now a smooth, marble-sized piece of cannabis resin.

Oh, Christ! Oh no! I'd completely forgotten I hadn't smoked it all and I knew, at that moment, my life was over. I would be dragged to the ground by ferocious beagles just seconds from now. Arrested by armed law enforcers who were already climbing down zip wires from helicopters hovering above the airport, from which all flights had been cancelled. I would be imprisoned for life for drug smuggling and forced to share a cell with a frustrated sumo wrestler recently convicted of mass murder. I shared the truth of our situation with my girlfriend, who simply told me to get rid of it. Leaving her seething in the queue, off I shot, a catastrophising loser in desperate search of a bin.

But I couldn't find a bin. Even if I could, how on earth would I be able to extract the 'marble' from my pocket and slip it in unnoticed? It would be too much of a risk to breach the huge six-inch gulf between the two, which I worked out was about as close as I would have been able to get my hip to the rim without looking very weird. Anyway, I was almost certainly under surveillance and had to act now. There was no other option—I must make my way to the loos, head down but at the pace of a casual shopper with all the time in the world. Once in, unless the sharpshooters had already made their way into the concourse from the rooftops, the evidence would be gone in seconds. It was now or never. I looked up once to check the floors above. The snipers were not there, yet. However, what was there, directly above my head, was a sign telling me that I was already, in fact, standing outside the toilets.

Small mercies. I made my way in, avoiding eye contact with all other inmates, and shot directly into a cubicle. With the door locked I knew I could hold off the law enforcement officers for a couple of minutes, and no kind of dog could get to me. Unless you include a Chihuahua, for example, which might be able to slip under the door. However, I didn't believe (and I stand by this) it would have offered a huge amount of threat, no matter how determined. I removed the marble from my pocket and was about to flush it down the loo when it suddenly struck me: *does cannabis float?* If so, then it would stay in the pan, bobbing away like evidence sitting on a gold platter for those terrifying law enforcement officers, who would no doubt fling me to the floor to acquire the cross-match resin samples from my pockets. I just couldn't take that risk, so I did something completely mad— I started to eat the bloody thing. I think a part of me felt it was a waste of a perfectly good piece of 'dope' to just dump it. I think my twisted and panicked mind also felt sorry for it. It deserved to be eaten.

I stood there, in the cubicle, taking tiny nibbles out of it as if I was some sort of squirrel or other rodent nibbling on a nut. It was absolutely disgusting and incredibly difficult to swallow. And I had no water. Realising this could take a very long time, I started to panic, again. What I don't understand even to this day is why, at this point, the consequences of what I was doing did not dawn on me. I just continued to nibble, more and more of the cannabis collecting on and between my teeth, creating a foul and accumulating black paste. I was turning myself into a highly conspicuous pirate. I decided to speed up the process and bite off two or three bigger lumps and swallow them whole. Alas my mouth and throat were becoming excruciatingly dry, which made swallowing almost impossible. Then I suddenly remembered I had a stick of chewing gum in my other pocket. I took it out and thrust it into my mouth. The cool minty taste was a shot of joy and relief and caused me, instinctively, to shove the rest of the cannabis into my mouth. I then immediately realised I have a paranoid thing about swallowing gum, and the two were now becoming irrevocably meshed.

So, with time pressing, and the thought of my girlfriend combusting in the queue, I decided the time had come to man up and leave this godforsaken place because either way I was probably dead anyway. I slowly opened the cubicle door and, with eyes fixed straight ahead, went up to the mirror to check my teeth. As subtly as possible, I pulled back my lips over my gums to expose my teeth. It was a miracle. A by-product of introducing gum into the equation was that it had instantly removed the cannabis from my teeth and, at least as it seemed to me at that moment, had actually given them quite a good clean. With a small surge of confidence (who would think to check the gum in my mouth?) and with the sudden idea of starting a new range in cannabis-infused chewing gum called Minty High (where 'getting stoned is a breath of fresh air') I made my way out and headed back towards the check-in desk.

The next twenty-five minutes went by remarkably smoothly, including avoiding my girlfriend's wrath by reaching her just before we were called to the desk. She punched my arm and told me I was a stupid idiot but that's nothing compared to what she might have done, and at least I also avoided being shot by a sniper. I felt strangely chilled as we passed through passport control and security and at that point it didn't occur to me that: a) I was afraid of flying b) I was currently eating cannabis in the form of chewing gum c) I was about to suddenly become exceedingly paranoid.

Once through to the departures lounge, things started to take a turn for the worse. I suddenly 'came up'; in other words, a rush of overwhelming energy, thought and emotion poured over me and then quickly congealed into sheer panic. It was as if someone had given me LSD, such was the potent force unleashed by a highly combustible mix of feeling very high but in the wrong place. You're not supposed to be off your face in a place you can't escape from, particularly when the only way out is on a plane— which at the best of times you hate going on. I entered an episode of complete terror and remember telling my girlfriend that I wanted my mummy, which for all sorts of reasons didn't go down well. Her repeatedly telling me to get my act together felt like shards of ice dropping through me, when what I needed was to be taken to a darkened room and put into bed. All she saw, of course, was a moron walking along, trying to press his face against cold walls to hide from the overwhelming sights and noise of people (not off their face) shopping, eating and drinking. It was all too bloody noisy and bright, and I just really, really wanted to be lying in a flotation tank.

My propensity to catastrophise, coupled with my already fragile mental health, fired up the marble of cannabis coursing through my veins and sent me off the Richter scale. And then our plane was delayed. That was the final straw. I proceeded to spend the next two and a half hours cubicle-hopping between toilets, huddling on loo seats. Yet, I am proud to say that even in the midst of acute paranoia, I never stayed in one cubicle for too long as I didn't want to leave people waiting outside, buttock-clenched in shart-infested waters. An omen perhaps. I was also very worried about drawing too much attention to myself and was convinced that darting furiously between loos was the best way to remain under the radar. My girlfriend continued to support me by pretending she didn't know me, which, looking back, I fully understand.

When finally it was time to board she did agree to hold my hand, which was very kind of her. If I'm honest, she was probably worried I would go completely mad and she wanted to get home to the UK. She needed to keep me as calm as possible. This worked quite well until we boarded the plane, which suddenly appeared to me, as I stood in the gangway, to be extremely thin. How on earth could people fit in there? I also couldn't understand how the walls of the plane could possibly keep out cloud and sky when up in the air. As she led me to my seat, she whispered to me, asking if I was ok, to which I replied, very loudly, "Stop shouting". Thankfully for everyone, when I finally took my seat and my girlfriend strapped me in, I apparently passed out.

***

I have been reflecting on my third significant, character-building Lisbon memory in the ANA business lounge, which I alluded to at beginning of this chapter. I've decided that since it is in many ways a poor cousin to my delightful adventure in the South of France, I will condense the highlights for you in the form of bullet points. The reason I mention these deeply embarrassing experiences at all is to make an important point. Heavy drinking, without question, takes its toll on your body. I am living proof. It happened to focus its particularly nasty assaults on my digestive system, but also on my blood pressure (now normal) and my short term memory. My memory had definitely started to lose its elasticity. Though it is far, far better now, I often wonder if irreparable damage might have been done, even at a very subtle level. The old weed won't have helped either. Even if I remain remarkably intact, the following incident is one which I'm very glad does not happen to me anymore…

- After a busy two days working in Lisbon, I was sitting in the crowded ANA Business Lounge, sipping a glass of red wine whilst looking at planes taking off and landing. Something stirred within me that felt like a giant, slippery worm. There was no doubt that I had to make my way immediately to the loos.

- I attempted to cross the business lounge with a slow, casual confidence because I thought that was expected of people travelling in business class. This vanity proved to be my undoing.

- Three-quarters of the way across the lounge, the giant, slippery worm made its inexorable way towards the light. I stopped to clench. I was certain the worm's head had been trapped in some sort of arm lock. That said, one of the problems with suddenly stopping in the middle of an airport business lounge and not moving a muscle is that it's a conspicuous act. As if you've just set up on a street corner near Covent Garden and assumed a specific position, like one of those living statues. I needed to move on. Taking very small steps, I minced the rest of the way over to the loos.

- As I stepped through the main door, I inadvertently relaxed that arm lock. I think I had a sense of having arrived, as one does when getting home and just collapsing on the sofa. However, I'd experienced this phase of anticipative loosening before, when cubicles are but mere feet away and I know that I would make it, regardless.

- As the worm caught its breath, regained its composure and began once more its rapid descent, I made my way to the nearest cubicle. I find this bit quite thrilling, living slightly on the edge; the having to dash adds to the sense of blissful relief when the moment comes.

- The cubicle was occupied. As was the one next to it, and the one next to that. Indeed, all six cubicles were occupied. Usually under these circumstances, even though the point of no return feels as if it has been reached, the re-establishing of the arm lock can prove successful *if* the right force is applied with the right level of determination. In other words, all is not lost.

- Unfortunately, all was lost. Well, nearly. It's amazing how much you can get done in a very short period of time when you put your mind to it.

- Thus, as the worm was being counted in before going live, I managed to scan the entire bathroom. All urinals were vacant, as was every sink. No one was in the loos except those in the cubicles. Logic dictated a dash to the sinks, because the one on the far left would, briefly at least, put me out of sight of anyone entering the loos.

- Just as I began the process of lowering my trousers and reversing, one of the cubicle doors opened. I had a split second to make up my mind; would I unleash in situ, or sprint into the now-vacated cubicle, risking the opening of the floodgates?

- I decided on the latter. The jury is out to this day as to whether this was the right decision.

- With my trousers and pants now moving rapidly down over my knees, my backside landed on the seat in the nick of time. The worm found its freedom, and I a profound feeling of relief. Pride, too, at the velocity of its exit.

- I sat there for a moment and laughed at myself. *What a jerk I am*, I thought. *But give me due credit, I'm bloody inventive when forced to act.*

- Then I looked down.

- The worm had exited a second earlier than I thought; only its main body had made it to the toilet bowl. The trousers had carried the head and neck with them down my legs.

- To make matters worse, my overnight bag and coat were on the seat where I'd left them. I had no choice. I would have to walk back across the business lounge in just my pants, shirt and shoes. I'm not sure why I felt I had to wear my shoes.

- In a moment of clarity, I took back control and removed my trousers. I then held them in the bowl of the loo, and while continuously flushing, scrubbed furiously as the water rushed over them in momentary bursts.

- I have no idea what all this sounded like beyond the walls of the cubicle, but within five minutes I'd successfully given my trousers, by hand, what I believed was the full washing machine experience: the spin, the soak, the tumble and—for extra measure—the mighty squeeze.

- I consigned my pants to one of my trouser pockets and proceeded to haul, tug and yank my wet trousers up and on. Allowing my shirt to hang loose over my backside, I stepped out of the cubicle. I didn't look at anyone at all, eyes fixed straight ahead, jaw clenched, barely breathing, until I'd reclaimed my possessions in the lounge. I pretended I was a machine, a robot programmed to collect forgotten bags and coats.

- Once I collected these items, I knew I must then shower and change into spare clothes, because these were the sole instructions being transmitted from the onboard computer currently controlling my every move.

- Unfortunately, this meant queuing up to purchase a towel, shampoo, and soap. There were about three people in front of me and I was standing there in wet trousers and a long shirt. I know I looked stupid.
- Then I remembered I was a robot which, if I just followed the logic to its conclusion, meant I could not possibly feel stupid.
- Towel duly purchased, I proceeded to the shower rooms, showered, put on fresh clothes and changed back into being human.

This was both good and bad, turning back into a human being. Good, because I would now be able to have a cold lager and console myself. Robots don't drink alcohol. Bad, because, as a human, I would have to relive time and again, throughout the rest of my life, what had just happened to me.

Chapter 10

Sober Socials

My first sober social took place in Manchester in February 2019, in the rather lovely Indian restaurant, Dishoom. These socials are designed to give members of Club Soda, who are either mindfully drinking or not drinking at all, the chance to meet other like-minded people to socialise in bars and restaurants without drinking alcohol. That can be pretty challenging, if you think about it: to be dependent on alcohol, make the decision to go out and meet with strangers in a place where lots of alcohol is available, and yet not drink.

As I stood on the platform waiting for my train to Manchester, that sense of being a lone hero descended upon me again, as it had done a few weeks back in Brick Lane. I imagined I was Liam Neeson in the film The Commuter—it seemed to fit the bill—boarding a train where my skills as a deadly sales insurance man would be called upon to kill... bottles of wine. That sense of being Liam was still with me as I boarded, but unfortunately it came to a grinding halt directly outside those convex loo doors on the train (which slide open far too widely and for far too long) due to a tremendous number of people stacked up in front of me. I pulled the reserved seat ticket out of my pocket, like a gun, and started to make my way through the crowd to my designated carriage. The carriage looked packed, but I had my seat ticket and I wasn't in the mood to be messed around. I even smugly said to someone who was pressed up against a window that I had a reserved seat, "So I'm going in." They wished me luck with an even more smug smile. The carriage doors opened and I was immediately hit by two quite distinct forces. One was the very loud singing in unison of around thirty men between the ages of eighteen and thirty. They were singing the highly complex ditty 'Ole, Ole, Ole' repeatedly and with huge gusto. The other 'force' was that of the stench of beer. This was quite ironic, all things considered. It was about 11.30am on a Saturday and I was off to a sober social, standing in a carriage with nearly thirty drunk men. That sense of being Liam was by now a distant memory as was the notion of making my way through the carriage to my seat, which was occupied by the enormous bloke leading the singing.

I did quietly laugh to myself at how ridiculous this was. A few things went through my mind as I stood there watching this scene of comedy and menace being played out in front of me. My first thought was that I could probably drink most of them under the table. Second, how many of them might one day end up as I did? Third, wouldn't it be funny if I did try to make my way to my seat regardless and stood there in front of the very large bloke sitting in my seat, surrounded by the thirty drunk blokes, who were all up for a 'bit of banter', and said:

"Hi there, completely understandable error, but you're actually sitting in my seat. Here, look, you're welcome to see my seat reservation if you wish, so would it be okay if we did a swap? And also, chaps, I wondered if you'd considered the impact that your very loud singing and drunkenness has had on the other travellers both here in the carriage, and also now inconveniently holed up in the gangways in front of the loo, exit doors and beyond? They too have seats reserved... Yes, that's right—where you're all currently sitting. Could we all do an exchange? Oh, and I know this is a slightly mad suggestion, but instead of going to the Stoke match, I wondered if you might like to accompany me to what is called a 'sober social'. There are many held throughout the country. I myself am on my way to attend one in Manchester, so you can see the rather amusing situation I find myself in, but, if I'm honest, perhaps there was a reason for our all meeting here today. A sign. So, I'll leave it entirely up to you, but if you just go onto Facebook, you'll see a link to Club Soda Together. It's what is called the Mindful Drinking Movement. In the

meantime, shall we all stand up... that's it, good fellows...
And I can direct you now, one by one, to the areas outside
the loo as we move the legitimate people from out there into
here. It should take no more than a few minutes. What do
you think?"

An hour later we were pulling into Manchester.

Clearly, the boys didn't take up my offer because I didn't
ask them. They had alighted at Stoke fifteen minutes after
I'd composed my speech, thank God. As we 'legitimate'
travellers watched, squeezed up against the windows as
the singers filed off one by one, I was struck by how
sheepish and lacking in confidence they all looked when
'alone': no longer part of a gang, but forced by the
narrowness of the train to be singular at that moment. Still,
I'm glad I didn't ask them to swap.

As I set off on the twenty-minute walk from Piccadilly station
to Dishoom, I started to envisage the next two hours ahead
of me. I had seen the list of people attending on the group's
event page; there would be about eighteen of us, three of
whom, including myself, would be men. Club Soda knows
that "...members, social media audiences and the general
population of mindful drinkers are comprised of a larger
percentage of women than men", and I guess that's to be

expected. Women are, by and large, more likely to share and connect when it comes to vulnerability in all its guises. I wondered what kind of man, therefore, is more likely to take the plunge and embrace the 'power of vulnerability', as Brené Brown encourages? It's about time more did because alcohol does not discriminate when it comes to gender and its ability to take hold. Living with it in silence is the force that drives the downward spiral.

Two minutes out from Dishoom, as I zigzagged down side streets, I scrolled one more time through the list of group members who'd marked themselves as 'Going' to the event, and tried to connect as many names to faces as I could. To be able to memorise some of them might mean my not looking entirely bewildered as I did the old "Hello, how do you do, I'm Simon, and you are?" thing, whereupon their name goes in one ear and immediately bounces out again before even remotely hitting the brain.

As I went down the list, I realised the men had gone.

I panicked and scrolled up to the Going, Maybe, Not Going tabs. The truth stared me in the face. Both men had bailed out! One had posted their apologies, but they felt too overwhelmed to attend this time, which I do understand. The other one had changed their Going setting to Not

Going without explanation. Great! There I was, entering Dishoom, knowing that it was going to be just me, stone-cold sober, meeting a dozen or so women who were probably already bonding.

Stepping through the door, I thought, for some reason, there would be someone there to greet me as if I was royalty or something—the special person who doesn't drink anymore. But of course the place wasn't going to be hired out especially for a dozen or so strangers to meet and not drink alcohol. I looked around. It was a lovely place, busy and classy with a nice bar area to my left, people at elegant tables to my right, and beyond, the restaurant itself. I made my way to the bar towards a group of about nine women all seated on stools, their backs to me, watching cocktails being made. "God, I really hope it's the Soda crew or I'm going to look like a complete idiot," I thought to myself as I approached.

Mind you, I think I looked like a complete idiot anyway with my rucksack over my shoulder (smaller even than the one in the south of France) and my 'I'm not sure how to dress for something like this' long-sleeved polo shirt contraption, and, I realised, trousers which were exactly the same colour as the top, making me look like I was part of a weird cult. I remember fretting that they'd probably think I'm some sort of entertainment, Mr. Blue Man, laid on by Club Soda.

I stopped behind them all and smiled an inane smile at the barman who was making the cocktails, which were, of course, mocktails. Phew. The ladies all turned as one and for a moment I felt like I was on Take Me Out and the barman was going to call out "No likey, no lighty." One of the women, the organiser for that day, smiled and asked me if I was there for the sober social. I confirmed as such and she kindly welcomed me, gesturing to me to pull up a stool. There I was, suddenly, squeezed into the middle of everyone: me, Mr Blue Man sitting amongst a gathering group of women, watching a barman make the most exotic mocktails and talk us through the details of each ingredient as he added them with surety, wit, and youth. I realised he was, in fact, the entertainment.

As we passed the mocktails around for tasting, I started chatting to some of my fellow sodas. It was a pretty surreal experience being plunged straight into mocktail tasting, passing glasses around to sip from, with people I didn't know, who were all there to learn to socialise without drinking alcohol. Not that I wanted us to have all gathered first in a quiet room to announce our names and say we had or had had an issue with alcohol dependency (or to start chanting), but perhaps something in the middle? A sort of quiet hello in private before hitting the bar?

Anyway, we were where we were, and I did slightly surprise myself with the fact that I was quite social. I mean, I am ordinarily, but I wasn't sure that I would be in a setting like this, under these circumstances. I'd worried about feeling an unsettling level of stress at not being able to drink when out with people I didn't know. The kind of restlessness I used to feel in my drinking days, when I was forced not to drink because I was the designated driver, for example. But I didn't feel that stress. I noticed some quiet people amongst us, who looked a little overwhelmed, but for me, the coming together with other non-drinkers was actually quite liberating.

What I liked was the fact that within minutes of starting a conversation with someone, we would start talking about the very thing that connected us. We'd discuss our relationship with alcohol, what it was like to be here doing this, how much we used to drink, that sort of thing. It was great to connect so immediately and openly about something so personal. Something that most of us had all, individually, held onto privately for so many years. Secretly. Painfully.

Simon Eastwood

The conversations carried on as we moved through to the restaurant for lunch, either one to one, in threes, or more, across the table, to my left and right. Intimate experiences being 'thankfully' shared and normalised by (and to) people who understood. And here's the important thing for me—we were doing it all in a place that served alcohol. Not in a special room for the special people who have an issue with addiction, but in a 'normal' place where 'normal' life is going on all around. In this situation, you learn, on the job, to adjust your own personal antenna to socialising in places you used to get plastered in. You learn to let the world around you do its thing while you do what you need to do. Happily.

I then started to do something I've done on each of the two subsequent sober socials I've attended—try to imagine what we would all look like completely trashed. I mean, how hysterical, in a morbid kind of way, because looking at all the dignity and grace around the table, I knew it would all have been very messy had you transported our previous selves into this moment. There would've been far more general physical 'sprawling', the tremendous upright poises before me replaced by elbows gradually lowering to the point where we would all eventually look like we were preparing to crawl under the table.

I would have loved for us to each have had a before and after photo—the one we would be taking now, and one from the good old days—to show how far we had come. In fact, when I come to think of it, it might be a rather therapeutic element to add to these sober socials. Creating a forum for us all to share the funniest and the most excruciating things that happened to us when we were riding the highways of Alcohol World. To laugh and to cry at the madness of it all, to bring out those 'snaps' and pass them round the table, to show everyone who we were then and all the ridiculous things we got up to. A kind of Comedy Store for the once dependent or perhaps rather a confessional. Or both.

The second Manchester Social I attended took place about five months later, only a ten-minute walk from Dishoom. This time the meet was in an all-out bar. A bit more down and dirty, a live band playing, tables full of people drinking, and, once again, a table for us little sodas to bond. There were largely new people but the same instant connection and discussion. All very different people, from different walks of life, sitting together sharing stories which reassuringly all had the same plot lines. It was good to see a few blokes there too this time, and I was taken by one or two of their bitter/sweet stories: how they'd lost everything, their money and their families to alcohol, but were slowly reconnecting with their children after years in the wilderness

170

and finding employment once again. Living alone, but doing things like this. Coming out to meet people a bit like them, dressed immaculately (much better than my cult outfit from February), and making an effort to live their lives again the right way.

I felt a sense of deep sadness and hope at the same time as I listened. How close had I been to losing everything? My dependency had been a slow burner, a flame travelling along a very long cord fuse, which I'd managed to put out in the nick of time, before the inevitable explosion which had unfortunately engulfed my two new friends.

And amongst all this, some powerful themes emerge about the relationships members have with others back in Alcohol World. One scenario that really stands out is the maintenance (or not) of the relationship with the partner, husband or wife who has remained a heavy drinker. This one comes up a lot. Very often, alcohol has defined the relationship for years; it quite possibly played the role of matchmaker in the first place. Sometimes alcohol is like a mutual friend who has, over time, become an ever-growing presence in a couple's lives—a lodger who begins to take over the family home because the owners have retreated into their separate parts of the house and only ever meet when the three of them get together. But now, one out of husband, wife or partner has chosen to stop drinking, but the lodger has stayed. Not only stayed, but moved in permanently with the one who did not stop. They are now an item and so life has become intolerable. For me, if this continues, there really is only one option.

But above all else, having spent time with people who have walked the same path as I from Alcohol World to Sober Land, I have learned that life is what we feel. And you have to ride it like the wonderful, exhilarating, overwhelming wave it is, which rises high and then suddenly dips. But while you stay sober you just keep riding it. And in the riding of it, you start to master it as a surfer does, one day at a time. It's only when you drink that you truly fall because at that moment you give up on feeling. So you climb back on board and start again, sober. And finally, you understand that the only way to keep riding that wave, at least for me, is to fully embrace it, to completely accept that those dips, which seem to consume you, are all part of the internal life experience of being human. Just as are those incredible naturally created highs that alcohol can never get close to emulating.

Chapter 11

The Shrinking

It's now early November 2019 and I am back in Wiltshire to see my mum. About six weeks ago, I took her to the local hospital for a review of a CT scan she'd had on her brain back in July, to get to the bottom of her increasing memory loss. It's not surprising, therefore, that when I arrived, she'd completely forgotten the reason why I had come down to see her. She thought it was because we were going out to that French bistro again and to do some early Christmas shopping. I told her it was that, too, and of course I would be taking 'the orangutan' out for dinner, but that tomorrow we would be going to the hospital to find out what all this memory loss thing was about.

We did the night out, the dodging of the puddles, the meal, the wine, the mint tea for me, the circular conversation, the mighty trek to the loo, the putting to bed with a glass of water and of course a glass of wine, the only medicine now taken. The closing of the apartment door and the hoping she would be alright.

I arrived back in the morning, where the carer was already getting her ready for our trip to the hospital, mum washed, dressed, and confused. All that happened and then it was time to go.

As I hoisted her once more out of her wheelchair and into my car, and as we made our way to the hospital, she asked several times where we were going and why. The same when I hoisted her back into her wheelchair and pushed her onwards towards the hospital entrance. Her white hair was up and dancing on her skull again as we crossed the car park, and I wondered what was going through her mind at that very moment. I have tried to imagine this more and more, recently. I have a sense that living like that must be like watching, constantly, a carousel at a fairground. Thoughts appear and no sooner have they appeared, like those grand horses, they've gone again. As you try to watch them leaving, another thought appears, and this is repeated until the first thought returns and so on. Round and round, unable to stop that carousel. Unable to bring it to a halt, to climb on board and walk around it, to scrutinise the intricate colours, to feel the smoothness of the wood and metal, to listen to the conversations of those around you and take in what they are really saying, or to perhaps climb up and on one of those horses, just look out at the world around you, and see it as it actually is. It must be so very, very frustrating.

We entered the hospital, checked in and made our way to the Neurology department. Thankfully, we were quickly called and moments later there we were, sitting in front of the doctor. She was very nice but for some reason I always feel I've been called in to see a school principal when I'm in front of a doctor. I turn into a very well-behaved child who is trying to impress. Meanwhile, I noticed my mother was also trying to impress, tidying up her hair and smiling her nicest smile. It reminded me of what she used to do when she was much younger—her looks were her most important asset, and old habits die hard. However, it was the other habit, which had not died at all, which had brought us here today.

At least, this was what was about to be confirmed.

The doctor looked at her notes for a while and then looked up and said to my mother, with a kindly smile, "How much alcohol do you drink, Mrs Eastwood?"

My mother hesitated and I couldn't work out whether that hesitation was down to her struggling to recall how much she drank, or whether she was just taken aback. I was quite taken aback myself, I have to say. So, while my mother desperately searched her mind for the answer—did she mean daily, weekly or monthly?—I simply asked, very nicely, what the reason was for the question, out of interest. The doctor replied that she could see, looking at the notes from my mother's last assessment, that she appeared to drink quite heavily, and that her query was relevant to the scans she had reviewed. She said all this with warmth and understanding and so I felt compelled to answer honestly on behalf of my mother. I told her that my mother consumed about eight bottles of wine a week and a litre of sherry.

"Oh, it's not that much, Simon," my mother said indignantly.

"It is, Mum."

"Don't be silly, of course it's not. It's not all for me."

"Who else is it for, Mum?"

"I have people around. I have guests. I don't have it all."

"You do, Mum. You don't have any guests around who drink your wine or sherry. And you always run out just as the new order comes in—which I order for you." I felt I sounded cruel, saying this out loud.

"Well, that's just silly," my mother said under her breath.

The doctor and I smiled at each other and then she turned to her screen, shifted it so we could both see it properly, and proceeded to 'play' the scan of my mother's brain to us. How very bizarre, I thought, watching my mother's brain appear on the screen whilst looking at her head perched on her shoulders right next to me. I kept flicking between the two like a mesmerised dog looks at a ball being thrown between two people. I was trying to picture that brain in that head. I realised we were beaming in from the top of my mother's skull and zooming down. As the brain came fully into view, the doctor talked us through the findings.

"So, that's where the atrophy is... The shrinkage."

"What is all that?" my mother said.

"It's your brain, Mother."

"And that's where the fluid is, that's the ventricles," the doctor continued.

"Is that my brain?"

"Yes, it is indeed your brain, Mother."

"Good lord. I actually have a brain," she said.

I laughed out loud at that, as did the doctor. Good for you, Mum, I thought. Humour is going to be the best medicine we can take from now on in. The doctor said that she'd consulted with a colleague and specialist about whether the atrophy was due to Normal Pressure Hydrocephalus (NPH), which is an accumulation of cerebrospinal fluid (CSF) that causes the ventricles in the brain to become enlarged. However, what the imaging showed was not in keeping with this; what they were seeing was more of a generalised atrophy. I asked the doctor what all this meant. She turned and said quietly, and only to me, that some of the 'wear and tear' would be just down to old age but the significant shrinkage or atrophy was down to chronic alcohol use.

To hear someone else say this out loud, directly to me, was overwhelming. At that moment I felt my entire life since childhood rush over me; the truth that had hidden in plain sight was out. In fact, my mother's dependency on alcohol was not hidden but, as is often the case with the heavy-drinking family member or friend, was always laughed off or made light of. Not ever actually named. Never actually dealt with.

I feel I have to say something at this point in case any of my family or my mother's friends should ever read this. I have of course gone back and forth about whether to include this very personal account. In no way do I so to offend or upset. However, I do feel that this moment is important to share; I think it makes a relevant point about how the effects of alcohol abuse, over a sustained period, are not only very real but are more commonplace than one might think. The extreme effects of long-term heavy drinking aren't limited to the people we see on park benches, drinking vodka out of bottles hidden in paper bags: the people with that unmistakable 'look' which separates them from the rest of us. At least so we think. My mentioning this is about opening the eyes of ordinary people living perfectly ordinary lives. The results are gradual, understandable, and my account of the potential consequences is absolutely not about blame.

Next, the doctor asked my mother if she could do a few memory tests on her. I started to panic. Not for my mum, but for me! What would happen if, as I listened on, I would be unable to remember what my mother was being asked to remember? What would happen if my alcohol consumption, over all those years, had also resulted in my own brain having shrunk?

I steadied myself as the doctor began the test, trying desperately to focus whilst catastrophising about the fact that both my mother and I would soon be moving into a care home together. The moment of truth had arrived.

My mother started off quite well and was able to name seventeen different animals in one minute. I was also trying to reel off names of animals at the same time in my head, but my levels of stress were so high my mind kept going blank. And then I panicked that my mind going blank was because my brain was indeed filled with millions of blank spots, an atrophy-riddled brain working furiously to keep up with my mother's atrophy-shrunken brain. I then lost count of how many animals I managed to name.

Next, the doctor gave my mother three words to remember: lemon, key, and ball. I was determined to remember these three words so I resolved to do this by associating them with something ridiculous; I looked at the doctor and imagined she had a *lemon* sticking out of her mouth and when I turned the *key* in her ear a *ball* would drop out of one of her nostrils and the *lemon* would be sucked up into her mouth. When I turned the *key* back the other way the *ball* would disappear back up her nose and the *lemon* would reappear, sticking once more out of her mouth.

Next, the doctor asked my mother to name as many things as she could beginning with the letter P. This didn't go so well for my mother; for some reason, she became obsessed with trying to name only animals beginning with the letter P, even though the doctor and I kept telling her it could be anything she liked. She was able to name just seven things this time around. I didn't attempt this task because I was still busily turning the key in the doctor's ear and watching the lemon and ball moving in and out of her mouth and nose. The doctor then asked my mother to give the names of her grandchildren, of which she has five. She was able to name four. She wasn't able to name what month we were in or indeed what year.

The doctor then asked my mother to say the three words she'd been asked to remember. My mother remembered lemon. I remembered all three, which I was really chuffed about, but then started to obsess about whether I should have imagined the *ball* in the doctor's mouth and the lemon dropping out of her nostril because lemons are more nostril-shaped than balls, and balls fit more snugly in the mouth. It would have been far more logical to have pictured it this way. More memorable. I also wondered if I should have put the key in the middle of her forehead rather than her ear, as it would all then be perfectly aligned, with some sort of chain linking all three together.

My mother's final test was in relation to her walking. The doctor wanted to see her walk across the room because this too can apparently indicate whether someone has gait apraxia, where movement is impacted by bilateral frontal lobe disorders. Unfortunately, my mother felt unable to do this as she didn't have her Zimmer frame. So, for some ridiculous reason, I offered to demonstrate her walk. The problem was I did this far too literally, as if I thought I was auditioning for something, or taking a class in physical theatre. I cringe when I look back on this because I found the doctor quite attractive and had imagined that we might marry at some point in the future.

I got up from my chair and then assumed the orangutan position my mother gets into when being escorted. I think I even held my hand up over my head as if someone was holding it. I then proceeded to walk across the room, back arched, taking little stuttering steps, swinging my hips forward with each move to demonstrate that my mother would use the entire lower half of her body to swing each leg forward. I actually imagined I *was* my mother and therefore took a very long time to cross the room. I can't imagine what on earth the doctor was thinking (she was probably writing up her notes) but I did look up once at my mother, from my stooped position, and remembered thinking she looked totally bewildered.

After all that the doctor concluded that my mother's gait probably was not apraxic, which for some reason I felt quite offended about. We bade farewell to her and she said she would be writing to my mother's GP with her conclusions and recommendations. The bottom line was that the atrophy could not be reversed. However, my mother did still need to cut down on her drinking for general health reasons, and to ensure that she was as physically in control as she could be, let alone mentally. Fat chance of that happening, I thought, and my mother confirmed this as we made our way along the corridors of the hospital. The doctor would be recommending that B vitamins and analgesics be prescribed. My mother would be recommending Sauvignon blanc and sherry, "Because if I'm going ga-ga," she said, "what's the point in giving up now? I might as well enjoy it."

"Maybe you're right, Mum," I said, as I peered down on her white hair once more. It seemed somewhat flat at that moment, a little in keeping with how I was feeling. The thing was, that even if her brain did not hold much value for her anymore, the question of her ability to look after herself physically was still there.

I realised at that moment, seeing her being pushed along in her wheelchair, lost in her own world and barely able to walk now, that I needed to make efforts to get her into a care home sooner rather than later. She just wouldn't be able to cope much longer where she was and with the care she was currently receiving. It had to happen before it was too late.

As I lifted my mother once more out of her wheelchair and into the car, I took one last look back up at the hospital and said out loud the words 'lemon', 'key' and 'ball'.

***

About ten days ago I received a call from the warden where my mother lives to say she'd had another fall. This was the second in the space of a few weeks and the second time she'd been taken to hospital. This time she'd been on the kitchen floor for eight hours with a carer by her side because there were too many emergency call-outs that day. My mother's fall was finally deemed an emergency and an ambulance was sent. Our NHS is seriously stretched, is it not?

The time had come for me to act. I decided immediately to visit a care home closest to me, which I had been considering for a while, and to start the ball rolling with Adult Social Care. Blimey, that was an experience! If my mum goes into this care home, it's either going to be the making of her or it will send her up into the stratosphere, wine bottle in one hand, Zimmer frame in the other, and her white hair pointed to the heavens. Like hospitals, churches, Disney Land and the BBC (I used to work there), care homes are an entire world all of their own, aren't they? And I thought Sober Land was something to write home about.

I turned into the car park and there it was, the care home where my mother might be coming to live, appearing like a Premier Inn. Very neat and sensible-looking from the outside, with fields on three sides giving it a rather lovely aspect. When I walked into reception, however, I felt like I had stepped through some kind of portal; I was thrown straight into this busy and quite bonkers (I don't mean literally or at least not entirely) environment, possibly on another planet. There were lots of people doing lots of things, quite loudly, as it happens. I thought it was going to be all echoing corridors and whispered conversations amongst footsteps ringing out on steely floors or keys clanging as they turned in locks. Then I realised I was thinking of prison, or—worse—some maniacal institution in a horror movie.

The assistant manager of the care home came to meet me as arranged and then we were off on a whirlwind tour. On both the ground floor and first floor were bedrooms, a dining room, lounges, chill-out zones, a cafe, a games room, a hair salon and so forth. Blinking hell, it was a bit like some 65 to 95 holiday resort. As I passed down corridors, I saw snapshots of elderly people in different states of being—asleep in a chair or being lifted to their feet, sipping a glass of wine while watching television (must get the name of that gentleman for my mum on the way back) or simply sitting quietly and staring out over the fields.

Groups of them were singing in chairs lined up in front of a young woman or doing exercises for their gluteus maximus. Not the best thought to conjure up. I saw lunch being served, chess being played, coffee being taken and hair being cut, all with lots of chatting and laughing—a kaleidoscope of white hair, thin legs, and carers a-plenty, all creating a sense of continuous motion. I quite liked it. In fact, I did contemplate the idea of moving in myself.

Is this just the start? I thought. I pictured a future where almost all our money goes into our care for when we're old, so that entire cities can be built across the world for 'the old ones', where we all go one day. Self-driving electric vehicles taking us here, there and everywhere and each of us looked after by robot carers twenty-four hours a day. The rest of the world avoiding these cities for as long as they can, out of sight out of mind, just as I had the care homes of today, right up until that moment. I've always said that when I go, I don't want it to be in a care home but on my terms, like in Thelma and Louise. I picture myself in a car facing a cliff edge, just me, very old but still able to sit behind the wheel and there, by my side in the passenger seat, my very old dog. We look at each other once, he with his chew in his mouth, me with a bottle of alcohol-free lager in my hand (it used to be a bottle of vodka) and we smile. I readjust the photo on the dashboard of my now grown-up children and their families, turn up the music—Bat out of Hell would be quite good—push down on the throttle, wheels spinning, dust flying as friends and family wave us off, and then we're gone, speeding towards eternity.

So, why was I going to do this for my mum? Or *to* her, perhaps I should say? What would be her Thelma and Louise equivalent? For sure, she'd have a bottle of white wine in her hand, and she'd probably be sitting in the middle of a safari on the plains of Africa, wild animals all around her, looking up at the stars as she used to do with her first husband, when she was very young, living in Kenya. And here's the thing. My mother has always said to me that if she should ever 'lose her mind', she doesn't want to be just kept going or end up in a care home, seeing out her days on some conveyor belt. I understand that. But what choice do I have? What choice do any of us have when our parents can no longer look after themselves?

Last week I went to see her in hospital. She has now become extremely confused. She was going to be moved into a temporary care home in Salisbury for assessment, so I went to the room she would be moving into. I'd collected a few things from her little apartment, the apartment where eight bottles of wine and a litre of sherry had been delivered every week up until only a week ago. There were about four unopened bottles of Sauvignon blanc in a box and half a bottle in the fridge. I didn't touch them. They no longer had any use for me now. I packed some clothes, photos, toiletries and a backlog of Daily Mails and headed off. I tried to set up her new 'temporary' room as invitingly as I could, photos all around the room, clothes hanging in the cupboard, a Christmas card from me left on her bed with a rather forlorn bunch of flowers, and then I slipped away into the already darkening afternoon.

Chapter 12

Sober Land

When my sister Jenny died, my mother and I made a long and painful trip to Australia for her funeral. I am not sure, even to this day, just what this must have been like for my mother, and perhaps that is why, in part, I will always understand her relentless pursuit of alcohol. Yes, the lure had been there for as long as I can remember, but this experience would surely have enticed her past the point of no return. I often think about the impact of my sister's death on my nephews, too. The one in Australia has forged a good life for himself, of which I am most proud, yet still I want to reach out and see how he really is. And how about his younger brother in Spain? I hope that the adventures I've described in this book might resonate with him particularly. As I write this, my mother sits confused in her temporary care home, still being assessed, and I'm sitting here thinking about a life that has been spent largely out of control, hidden beneath a thin veneer of far too many smiles and too much assumed strength. Can you relate to this?

Mental illness is real, as real as any physical illness, and I am so glad that it is now being talked about with kindness and understanding. I wish this progression had begun earlier. Since I was teenager, I've lived with the burden of overthinking and overfeeling, and caring too much what others think of me because of my desperately low self-esteem. It doesn't matter why anymore; it just matters that I can say it out loud.

I never made the connection that I used alcohol and drugs to try to make it all go away for almost all my adult life. I thought you could only be classed as having a "real" drink and drug problem if you hit a huge and catastrophic rock bottom and were admitted into rehab or perhaps even sectioned. I didn't realise I had achieved this status secretly over a very long period of time. Was this true of my mother and my sister too? And indeed, others in my family? I often think human beings are caught in a cruel conundrum: too intelligent to stop asking why, but not quite intelligent enough to ever find the answer.

It's been well over a year since I last had a drink. The second of September 2018, to be precise.

Though I feel infinitely better, I can tell you that those difficult feelings are never far away. But by letting them in and no longer running from them, I've given myself the chance to find the peace of mind we all crave. All that lies between us and reality is our perception of it. Apart from the unavoidable things that happen to us, the rest of our life experience is down to how we feel or think from one moment to the next, and the choices we then make as a result.

I know that whatever new adventures should await (and I hope there are many), this time I will be doing them sober, and that's exciting. My children and my sobriety are what matter most to me; from that, the rest will follow here in Sober Land. After all, this is where we were all born wasn't it? This Sober Land? It's where we all come from. It's just that at some point many of us decided to leave and explore what we perceived as a far more exotic and tantalising place called Alcohol World. Some of us can journey back and forth without trouble or question. Some seem have those weekends away, or the odd overnight stay, down to a tee. Others of us don't. Many others.

So, I will end this by quoting John Lennon because I think this gives hope to us all, no matter where we might be on our travels towards sobriety—if that is what we want—as well as our seeking of that most elusive of places, mental wellbeing:

"Everything will be okay in the end.
If it's not ok, it's not the end."

John Lennon

Epilogue

April 2020.

As I sit here, looking back on what I have written, trying to conjure up some sort of conclusion to it all, the word Epilogue sounds far too grand for a book like mine. Since it's splattered largely in schoolboy humour and the ramblings of a catastrophiser, it would be far more apt, I think, to call it an Epic Log.

I have mentioned a few times in this book the need to accept uncomfortable feelings and to face up to them instead of drowning them (at least in my case) in copious amounts of red wine, only to find them bobbing up once more to the surface the following day like pieces of wreckage that refuse to sink.

I am so grateful, during this pandemic lockdown, that turning to alcohol is the last thing on my mind. That's how far I've come, and I hope this shows you or anyone you might know that it's entirely possible to break free from the need to deal with life using whatever your choice of drug might be. Even in the most stressful of times.

However, my issues with anxiety remain and I've learnt that the best remedy is in being able to reach out to friends and tell them how I'm feeling. I know that seems so simple and obvious, but for many, many years I did not. Look where that choice to keep my fears to myself took me.

Here in Sober Land I'm also able to reach out, online, to my fellow Club Soda members, and I am bowled over by the kindness and support everyone gives each other. We are all bound by the fact we were once dependent on alcohol, or that we still are, and that with guidance, we're making our way across the vast plains of Alcohol World to this new land. We all know what it is like to feel compelled to drink and can entirely relate to the reasons why we reached that point. That's what makes being part of this community of intimate strangers both so liberating and comforting.

And what of my mother? She has now returned to her little apartment in the warden-assisted complex. Her wonderful carers still come in four times a day to look after her, and the equally wonderful warden, Jane, goes out to get my mother her food and other supplies as she does for others in the block, going above and beyond to keep those there as safe and secure as possible. I can't thank them all enough.

The extraordinary thing is that my mother is not drinking alcohol. Not through choice, I'll have you know, but because I'm not really allowed to order her any. These are instructions from those that manage the apartment my mother lives in as well as the commands descending from general medical advice. My mother protests, of course, and I fairly regularly get blamed for cutting off her supply. The call comes in:

"Hi Mum, how are you?"

"I'm rather cross actually, Simon."

"Oh, why's that, mum?"

"You've stopped ordering me my wine and I don't have any and I am entitled to have some."

"I know you really want to have your wine, Mum. But I am not allowed to order you any."

"Why? Why can't you order me some?"

"It's the people who you rent your apartment from, and it's also what has been advised medically."

"But it has nothing to do with them."

"But it does, Mum."

"Why?"

"Because you keep falling over, Mum."

"That's ridiculous – I only fell over once and it's because I can barely walk."

"It was more than once—you had to go into hospital two times in quick succession. They feel it's too much of a risk."

"At my age I should be allowed to have a drink. I've been drinking all my life and I'm old enough to make my own decisions."

"I understand, Mum."

"All I want is to have a small glass of wine—it's not like I was drinking a lot."

"Okay, Mum. But the point is, I'm not allowed to order you any, but I have ordered you some alcohol-free—"

"It's since you stopped drinking that all this has happened."

"It's not, Mum, but I know how you must feel. I know you really like having your wine."

"It just gives me something to look forward to."

"I know. I understand that."

And the truth is I do understand. There is a part of me that really wants to give my mother what she wants in order to make her happy. One might argue that frankly she's reached a point in her life where, really, what difference does it make? And if it makes her happy, isn't that the important thing? Yet I was struck the other day by what Jane the warden said to me. She called me to say that it was quite amazing. My mother is no longer incontinent, and she looks so much better and healthier. Better than she has done for a long time. Her skin is glowing, she seems stronger. Ever since she stopped drinking. Jane sounded so pleased and excited by this transformation.

And that's just it. You're never too old. It's never too late to transform.

Here is an article I wrote before starting this book, which might be of interest:

The truth that hides in plain sight

Alcohol is no longer my friend, so I wanted to apologise up front to those who are actually on very good terms with it, if my views seem a little jaded. I guess it's inevitable that with some distance opened up between us, I should have developed a quite marked perception of this particular drug.

So, this is what I see. I see an act of extraordinary mass collusion. A collusion which enables alcohol to hide its truth in plain sight. As if by one giant sleight of hand, it has tricked large swathes of society into believing it's completely normal to use it to alter their minds and feelings in order to have a good time or deal with life. In that sense, you could say alcohol is borderline genius. To have managed to slip the net other drugs could not breach and then gone onto become one of the biggest players on earth. More influential than the wealthiest people, more controlling than the most powerful dictators. It makes fools of cocaine, heroin, and even marijuana, along with all other drugs which have to live their lives behind closed doors. These other drugs live dirty, sordid, high risk lives in shadows while alcohol struts into every corner of human life, gleaming in its beautiful and enticing bottles, or spread wide on billboards, chest puffed out and smiling the broadest, most smug smile possible.

It makes so much money for its hangers-on, too: its manufacturers, its marketeers, supermarkets, restaurants, bars and governments. They pander to its every whim as it works its way into everyday lives and starts to take hold. The still ridiculously cheap ticket to having so-called fun or, more worryingly, "dealing" with your feelings.

Except that, like any other drug, it often creates the very problems its users are trying to escape from. Feeling depressed? It will make you more so tomorrow. Anxious? Check. Need calming? Let's see what happens in a few hours' time. So, we then ingest more to try to reclaim feelings it has in fact taken away, and the cycle continues. And because it's legal, and not only socially acceptable but actively encouraged, so many of us don't stand a chance. If you have a chink in your armour, it will find its way in somehow. Eventually.

I take my hat off to those who really can take it or leave it when it comes to alcohol. They might have a glass of something every now and then, but weeks or months will pass when it never crosses their minds. They are the few who drink not to be happy but rather to be even happier. For the rest of us it's often a different story. We sit somewhere on the relationship spectrum with alcohol from 'just at the weekends' to 'every day'. And the relationship only ever gets stronger. What's disturbing is that the 'every day' is becoming the norm as well as the 'weekend binging'.

So, I just wanted to say to those of you who now find yourselves in the 'every day' category (or the binge section) and are secretly concerned about this, do not be ashamed. You are not alone, far from it, and you really can live a different, more joyful and exhilarating life without alcohol. If you wake up in the middle of the night with self-loathing, promising yourself that tomorrow you will not drink (but find yourself doing so come the evening), or having to fight exhaustedly not to, then be assured that it is absolutely possible to break that agonising cycle of behaviour.

It is perfectly understandable that you find yourself in this place. Alcohol is an addictive drug. It's a no-brainer that if you've used it habitually to enjoy occasions or to relax that it's going to take hold at some point. What we need to do is to start celebrating and admiring those who kick the habit, as we do those who do any other drug, instead of questioning them as to why they have and making them feel there must be something wrong with them. In fact, I'd wager alcohol is the hardest drug to quit of all because society pushes it at us from every side. So, double those brownie points.

I think it's time for society to stop colluding with this drug, to see it for what it is and to embrace wholeheartedly those who choose not to take it. I'm not saying we should make it illegal, or that we should preach incessantly about its harm on people's physical and mental health.

For now, all I ask is that we simply speak openly about its truth.

Acknowledgements

Thank you to everyone I have met through Club Soda Together, who are all living out their own particular adventures here in Sober Land. It's so much better when you travel together.

Those friends who have listened and been there when I have been at my most desperate—Miles, Phil, Janet and Mike in particular.

My mum, because despite everything I know you love me. And without you, I wouldn't have had so much great material for this book!

Printed in Germany
by Amazon Distribution
GmbH, Leipzig

18075131R00124